A Collection of Rare and Curious Tracts on Witchcraft and the Second Sight; With an Original Essay on Witchcraft.

By Various
Edited by Anthony Uyl

Woodstock, Ontario, 2016

A Collection of Rare and Curious Tracts on Witchcraft and the Second Sight; With an Original Essay on Witchcraft.
By Various
Edited by Anthony Uyl

Orginally Published By:
Edinburgh: Printed for D. Webster, 35, West College Street. 1820. Edinburgh: Printed by Thomas Webster.

 The text of A Collection of Rare and Curious Tracts on Witchcraft and the Second Sight; With an Original Essay on Witchcraft. is all in the Public Domain. The layout is not in the Public Domain and is Copyright 2016© Devoted Publishing a division of 2165467 Ontario Inc.

Let us hear your stories and thoughts!

Contact us at: devotedpub@hotmail.com
Visit us on Facebook: @DevotedPublishing
Visit our website for other Devoted Publishing books: www.devotedpublishing.com
Published in Woodstock, Ontario, Canada 2016.

ISBN: 978-1-988297-47-7

Table of Contents

Part I...4

   An Original Essay on Witchcraft..4

Part II..6

   News from Scotland: Declaring the Damnable Life of Doctor Fian, A Notable Sorcerer, Who Was Burned at Edenbrough in Januarie last, 1591...6

   A True Discourse of the Apprehension of Sundrie Witches Lately Taken in Scotland; Whereof Some Are Executed, and Some Are Yet Imprisoned.--With a Particular Recitall of Their Examinations, Taken in the Presence of the King's Magestie..7

   Footnotes:...11

   Another Account of the Foregoing Transactions, Extracted from Sir James Melvil's Memoirs, page 388, octavo edition...13

   Footnotes:...14

   Advertisement..15

Part III..16

   Extracts From King James's Daemonologie, Concerning Sorcery and Witchcraft......16

   Footnotes:...22

Part IV...23

   An Answer of a Letter from A Gentleman in Fife, to a Nobleman, Contaiting a Brief Account of the Barbarous and Illegal Treatment These Poor Women Accused of Witchcraft Met with from the Bailles of Pittenweem and Others--with some Observations Thereon..................23

   An Account of an Horrd and Barbarous Murder, In a Letter from a Gentleman in Fife to his Friend in Edinburgh...25

   A Just Reproof to the False Reports and Unjust Calumnies, in the Foregoing Letters........27

   Footnotes:...31

   A COPY OF THE INDICTMENT OF THE WITCHES AT BORROWSTOUNESS--THE PRECEPT FOR SUMMONING THE JURY AND WITNESSES--WITH THE WARRANT FOR THEIR EXECUTION..32

   Footnotes:...34

   TRIAL OF ISOBEL ELLIOT, AND NINE OTHER WOMEN.......................................35

   THE CONFESSIONS OF HELEN TAYLOR IN EYEMOUTH, AND MENIE HALYBURTON IN DIRLTON, ACCUSED OF WITCHCRAFT, 1649..36

   THE DEPOSITION OF MENIE HALIBURTOUN..37

   THE TRIAL OF WILLIAM COKE AND ALISON DICK, FOR WITCHCRAFT..............39

   Footnotes:...42

   MINUTES AND PROCEEDINGS OF THE SESSION OF TORRYBURN, IN FIFESHIRE, CONCERNING WITCHCRAFT. WITH THE CONFESSION OF LILLIAS ADIE................43

   Footnotes:...48

Part V..49

   ΔΕΤΤΕΡΟΣΚΟΠΙΑ; OR A BRIEF DISCOURSE CONCERNING THE SECOND SIGHT; COMMONLY SO CALLED..49

   A SHORT ADVERTISEMENT TO THE READER..52

   ΔΕΤΤΕΡΟΣΚΟΠΙΑ; OR, A BRIEF DISCOURSE CONCERNING THE SECOND SIGHT, Commonly so Called..53

Part I

An Original Essay on Witchcraft

If we wish to form a just estimate of the human character in its progress through the various stages of civilization, from ignorance and barbarism, to science and refinement, we must search into the natural causes that actuate the human mind. The life of man is prolonged to a remoter period, but subjected to more casualities, and greater vicissitudes of fortune, than most other animals. From these causes arises his anxious solicitude about futurity, and an eager desire to know his destiny; and thus man becomes the most superstitious of all other creatures. In every nation there have been multitudes of oracles, augurs, soothsayers, diviners, fortune-tellers, witches, sorcerers, &c. whose business has been to communicate intelligence respecting futurity, to the rest of mankind. If we attend to history, we shall find this theory sufficiently confirmed by experience. The most superstitious part of the species are soldiers and sailors, who are more exposed to accidents than any other class. History is full of the superstitious observances of the Roman armies; their regard to omens; the entrails of victims; the flight of birds, &c. and there are thousands of brave sailors of the present day, who would not sail in the finest ship of the British navy, without a horse-shoe were nailed on the main-mast. This passion of diving into futurity, naturally produced a number of 'dealers in destiny's dark council,' who soon found it turn out a very lucrative profession. From knowing the secrets, it was naturally inferred, that they were the favourites of those powers who are supposed to have the future happiness of mankind at their disposal. This we apprehend is the real source of that power which the priesthood hath ever exercised over the human mind. Pleasure and pain are the two great principles of human action which has given rise to the good and evil principle common to all nations. Those who held communication and commerce with the evil principle, are witches, wizzards, sorcerers, &c. Although we have various laws and injunctions against witchcraft in scripture, yet we are still as much in the dark as ever, as no definition is given of it, nor is the particular actions which constitute witchcraft enumerated, so as we can say wherein it consists. The story of the witch of Endor, is a case that throws more light on the subject than any other. But she appears to have acted more in the character of one of our second sighted seers, than one of our modern witches. According to our notions and ideas of witchcraft (as laid down by that sapient monarch James VI.), it is a poor ignorant old woman, who, through misery or malice, gives herself to the devil, soul and body, and renounces her baptism; for which considerations Satan engages to assist her with his power to work a number of petty mischiefs on such as she has a spite at; and sometimes he advances a little of the 'needful,' which, unfortunately for the poor old hag, turns out to be 'naething but sklate stanes,' and this most unaccountable contract is generally sealed by 'carnal copulation!' And yet, after believing this, we call ourselves rational creatures, and other animals we term brutes!! Many people have wondered, how so exalted a personage as the devil formerly was in days of yore, should latterly have taken up with such low company as our modern witches. He who tempted the very fathers of the church in so many various ways; who kept the whole priesthood of the Catholic church constantly on the alert with holy water, exorcisms, &c. only to keep him in check; who often attacked Luther and our other reformers, in very ungentlemanly disguises; and had even the audacity to insult our covenanted saints, by bellowing like a bull, grunting like a pig, or groaning like a dying man. These were pranks something worthier of a devil than the tricks played off by the witches. Our King James gives the reason, because 'the consumation of the world, and our deliverance drawing neere, makes Satan so rage the more in his instruments, knowing his kingdom to be so neere an end.' James was a little out in his reckoning here, 'the consumation of the world' not having taken place as yet, and the devil's kingdom turning out to be rather better established than his own. So far was it from being near an end, that it was on the increase, caused chiefly by the absurd and stupid laws that were enacted against it by himself and successors. The devil's kingdom is not to be destroyed by acts of parliament and burning of witches; these expedients have been tried in vain all over Europe and America, without effect; but now, when every person can bewitch with impunity, not a witch is to be found; and the devil, though left at large, has retreated to the Highlands and islands, where he is seldom seen, even by those who have the second sight. The true engines for battering the strong holds of Satan, and driving him and his imps into utter darkness, are science and philosophy; these are the weapons that have compelled him to retrograde movements, after lavishing rivers of holy water in vain. Thus the terrific claws of the devil, when seen by the distempered eyes of ignorant bigotry, appear to us truly horrible, but when viewed through philosophical spectacles, look as harmless as the lamb-skin gloves of a fine lady.

These stories, however, convey a strong likeness of the times in which they were acted. In our day, it is almost impossible to believe, that human beings could give credit to such gross absurdities as we have laid before the public in this little work, were the evidence not indubitable. Far less, that judges, lawyers, and divines, should unite in murdering such numbers of poor ignorant helpless creatures, for such mad chimeras, when it is hard to say, whether the poor victim, or the insane judges, were under the greater delusion. These wonderful tales of the doings of the devil with the witches, are taken from their own confessions, and from their delating of one another, as it is called. To us it does not appear improbable, but that too many of the poor deluded wretches actually imagined themselves to be witches. Nor will this appear so very surprizing, if we consider the circumstances of the case. At that period, any person who doubted of witchcraft, was looked upon as an athiest, and worse than mad; the whole country, from one end to the other, was continually ringing with tales of witches, devils, and fairies, with such other trash. Is it not then most likely, that people should dream about them? and is there any thing unnatural in supposing, that they should mistake these dreams for realities? as is evidently proved in several cases, and then confess, not the actions they really did, but the effects of their own disordered imagination. Moreover, when confined for this imaginary crime, they were tortured in all manner of ways, deprived of sleep, flung into water, and brodit, as they called it, being striped naked and searched for the devil's mark, in the most indecent manner. These confessions, after they were made, were nothing more than the wild ravings of a distempered imagination; and such a tissue of inconsistencies, as no person of the present day would listen to. An old woman in the Isle of Teree (as related by Mr Frazer, page 165), took in her head that she was in heaven no less, and had eat and drank there; and so firmly had the poor creature imbibed the notion, that it was with some difficulty she could be undeceived. A curious account of a pretended meeting with the devil, is given by a gentleman of Normandy, in the Memoirs of Literature for November 1711.

"The pretended meeting, about which those who believe they have been at it, relate so many extravagant things, is only in their imagination. I own, that some country people, especially shepherds, do now and then rub their skin with some narcotick grease or ointments, which cast them into a sound sleep, and fill their imagination with a thousand visions. When they are thus asleep, they fancy they see every thing that was told them concerning the devil's meeting, by their fathers, who were also shepherds, or wizards, if you will have me to call them so. Whereupon I will inform you of what I have been told by a country friend of mine, who pretended to have a mind to go to the devil's meeting with his own shepherd, who had the reputation of being a great sorcerer. Having frequently urged that shepherd to carry him thither, at last he obtained his desire. He went to him in the night at the appointed time. The shepherd immediately gave him something to grease himself withal. He took the grease as if he had a mind to rub his skin with it; but he desired that the shepherd's son, who was to go to the devil's meeting with his father, should anoint himself first. Which being done, that gentleman told the shepherd, that he should be glad to know what would become of the young man. Not long after, the young man fell fast asleep, and when he awaked, though he had not stirred from that place, he gave an account of every thing he thought he had seen at the devil's meeting; and even named several persons whom he pretended to have seen there. My friend perceived then, that what is commonly said of the devil's meeting was a mere fancy. I have told you this story, that you may impart it to your brethren, who being prepossest with popular errors about witchcraft, do frequently hang and burn poor wretches, whose crime does only consist in the weakness of their imagination."

A thousand more instances might be produced to show, that the devil hath no meetings any where, but in the perturbed brain of ignorant credulity. The history of superstition is however of great use; we there see its dangerous influence upon the peace and happiness of society--its degrading effects upon the character and manners of nations, in morality, literature, jurisprudence, and science. Theology seems to have been particularly infected with this pestiferous contagion. The clergy were generally in the front rank of witch-hunters, and through their influence, the most of them were put to death. In places where the minister was inflamed with a holy zeal against the devil and his emissaries, such as Pittenweem and Torryburn, the parish became a perfect hot-bed for the rearing of witches; and so plentiful a crop did it produce, that it appeared nothing else could thrive. But in places where the minister had some portion of humanity, and a little common sense, the devil very rarely set foot on his territories, and witchcraft was not to be found. Since the repeal of the statutes against witchcraft, several prosecutions have been instituted against witches, who were convicted and punished; but it was bewitching silly ignorant people out of their money, goods, and common sense, by pretending a knowledge of futurity--a power of relieving maladies in man or beast--or procuring the affection of some favourite swain to a love-sick maiden. The dupes of these impostors do not altogether escape, as they are made the laughing stock of their neighbours; and by these means even this trade is now nearly annihilated. Happily for our times, the refulgent brightness of philosophy and science, hath dispelled these dark clouds of benighted superstition, and left us in possession only of our natural powers and faculties, which are quite enough.

    EDITOR.

Part II

News from Scotland: Declaring the Damnable Life of Doctor Fian, A Notable Sorcerer, Who Was Burned at Edenbrough in Januarie last, 1591.

Which Doctor Was Register to the Devill that Sundrie Times Preached at North Barricke Kirke to a Number of Notorious Witches. With the True Examinations of the said Doctor and Withces, as they Uttered them in the Presence of the Scottish King.

Discovering How They Pretended to beWitch and Drowne His Magestie in the Sea Comming From Denmarke; With Such Other Wonderfull Matters as the like Hath Not Bein Heard at Anie Time.

Originally Published By:
Published according to the Scottish Copie.
Printed for William Wright.
Edinburgh: Re-Printed For D. Webster, 35, West College Street. 1820.

To The Reader:

The manifold untruths which are spred abroad concerning the detestable actions and apprehension of those witches whereof this historie following truely entreateth, hath caused me to publish the same in print, and the rather for that sundrie written coppies are lately dispersed thereof, containing that the said witches were first discovered by meanes of a poore pedlar travelling to the towne of Trenent; and that by a wonderfull manner hee was in a moment conveyed at midnight from Scotland to Burdeux in France (being places of no small distance), into a merchant's sellar there; and after being sent from Burdeux into Scotland by certaine Scottish merchants to the King's Majestie, that he discovered those witches, and was the cause of their apprehension; with a number of matters miraculous and incredible: all which in truth are most false. Nevertheless, to satisfie a number of honest mindes, who are desirous to be informed of the veritie and truth of their confessions, which for certaintie is more stranger than the common reporte runneth, and yet with more truth. I have undertaken to publish this short Treatise which declareth the true discourse of all that happened, and as well what was pretended by those wicked and detestable witches against the King's Majestie; as also by what means they wrought the same.

All which examinations (gentle reader) I have here truly published as they were taken and uttered in the presence of the King's Majestie, praying thee to accept of it for veritie, the same being so true as cannot be reproved.

A True Discourse of the Apprehension of Sundrie Witches Lately Taken in Scotland; Whereof Some Are Executed, and Some Are Yet Imprisoned.--With a Particular Recitall of Their Examinations, Taken in the Presence of the King's Magestie.

God, by his omnipotent power, hath at all times, and daily dooth take such care, and is so vigilant for the weale and preservation of his owne, that thereby he disappointeth the wicked practices and evil intents of all such as by any means whatsoever seeke indirectly to conspire any thing contrary to his holy will: Yea, and by the same power he hath lately overthrowne and hindered the intentions and wicked dealings of a great number of ungodly creatures, no better than devils; who suffering themselves to be allured and enticed by the Devil whom they served, and unto whom they were privately sworne, entered into the detestable art of witchcraft, which they studied and practised so long time, that in the ende they had seduced by their sorcerie a number of others to be as bad as themselves, dwelling in the bounds of Lowthen, which is a principall shire or part of Scotland, where the Kinges Majestie useth to make his cheifest residence or abode; and to the ende that their detestable wickednesse which they prively had pretended against the Kinges Majestie, the commonweale of that countrie, with the nobilitie and subjects of the same, should come to light. God of his unspeakable goodnesse did reveale and laie it open in verie strange sorte, thereby to make known to the world that their actions were contrarie to the lawe of God and the naturall affection which we ought generally to beare one to another. The manner of the revealing whereof was as followeth.

Within the towne of Trenent, in the kingdome of Scotland, there dwelleth one David Seaton, who being deputie bailiffe in the said towne, had a maid called Geillies Duncane, who used secretlie to absent and lie forth of her maisters house every other night. This Geillies Duncane tooke in hand to help all such as were troubled or grieved with anie kinde of sickness or infirmitie, and in short space did performe many matters most miraculous; which things, forasmuche as she began to do them upon a sodaine, having never done the like before, made her maister and others to be in great admiration, and wondered thereat: by meanes whereof the saide David Seaton had his maide in great suspition that shee did not those things by naturall and lawfull waies, but rather supposed it to be done by some extraordinarie and unlawfull meanes.

Whereupon her maister began to grow verie inquisitive, and examined her which way and by what meanes shee was able to performe matters of so great importance; whereat shee gave him no aunswere: nevertheless, her maister to the intent that hee might the better trie and finde out the truth of the same, did with the help of others torment her with the torture of the pilliwinkes upon her fingers, which is a grievous torture, and binding or wrinching her head with a cord or roape, which is a most cruel torment also, yet would shee not confess anie thing; whereupon they suspecting that shee had beene marked by the devill (as commonly witches are,) made diligent search about her, and found the enemies mark to be in her fore crag, or fore part of her throate; which being found, shee confessed that all her doings was done by the wicked allurements and entisements of the devil, and that shee did them by witchcraft.

After this her confession, shee was committed to prison, where shee continued a season, where immediately shee accused these persons following to bee notorious witches, and caused them forthwith to be apprehended, one after another, viz. Agnes Sampson, the eldest witche of them all, dwelling in Haddington; Agnes Tompson of Edenbrough; Doctor Fian, alias John Cuningham, master of the schoole at Saltpans in Lowthian, of whose life and strange acts you shall heare more largely in the end of this discourse.

These were by the saide Geillies Duncane accused, as also George Motts' wife, dwelling in Lowthian; Robert Grierson, skipper; and Jannet Blandilands; with the potters wife of Seaton; the smith at the Brigge Hallies, with innumerable others in those parts, and dwelling in those bounds aforesaid, of whom some are alreadie executed, the rest remaine in prison to receive the doome of judgement at the Kinges Majesties will and pleasure.

The saide Geillies Duncane also caused Ewphame Mecalrean to bee apprehended, who conspired and performed the death of her godfather, and who used her art upon a gentleman, being one of the

Lordes and Justices of the Session, for bearing good-will to her daughter. Shee also caused to be apprehended one Barbara Naper, for bewitching to death Archbalde lait Earle of Angus, who languished to death by witchcraft, and yet the same was not suspected; but that he died of so strange a disease as the phisition knewe not how to cure or remedie the same. But of all other the said witches, these two last before recited, were reputed for as civil honest women as anie that dwelled within the cittie of Edenbrough, before they were apprehended. Many other besides were taken dwelling in Lieth, who are detayned in prison until his Majesties further will and pleasure be knowne; of whose wicked dooings you shall particularly heare, which was as followeth.

This aforesaide Agnes Sampson, which was the elder witche, was taken and brought to Haliriud House before the Kinges Majestie, and sundrie other of the nobilitie of Scotland, where shee was straytly examined; but all the persuasions which the Kinges Majestie used to her, with the rest of his councell, might not provoke or induce her to confess any thing, but stoode stiffley in the deniall of all that was layde to her charge; whereupon they caused her to be conveyed away unto prison, there to receive such torture as hath been lately provided for witches in that countrie; and for as muche as by due examination of witchcraft and witches in Scotland, it hath lately beene founde that the devill dooth generally marke them with a privie marke, by reason the witches have confessed themselves, that the devill doth licke them with his tong in some privie part of their bodie, before he dooth receive them to bee his servants, which marke commonlie is given them under the haire in some part of their bodie, whereby it may not easily be found out or seene, although they bee searched; and generally so long as the marke is not seene to those which search them, so long the parties which have the marke will never confess anie thing. Therefore by special commandment this Agnes Sampson had all her haire shaven off, n each part of her bodie, and her head thrawane with a rope according to the custome of that countrie, being a payne most grievous, which they continued almost an hower, during which time shee would not confess anie thing untill the divel's marke was founde upon her privities, then shee immediately confessed whatsoever was demaunded of her, and justifiying those persons aforesaide to be notorious witches.

Item, the said Agnes Sampson was after brought againe before the Kinges Majestie and his councell, and being examined of the meeting and detestable dealings of those witches, shee confessed, that upon the night of Allhallow Even last, shee was accompanied as well with the persons aforesaide, as also with a great many other witches, to the number of two hundreth, and that all they together went to sea, each one in a riddle or cive, and went into the same very substantially, with flaggons of wine, making merrie and drinking by the way in the same riddles or cives, to the Kirke of North Barrick in Lowthian, and that after they had landed, tooke hands on the lande and daunced this reill or short daunce, singing all with one voice,

> *Commer goe ye before, commer goe ye,*
> *Gif ye will not goe before, commer let me.*

At which time shee confessed, that this Geillies Duncane did goe before them playing this reill or daunce, uppon a small trumpe, called a Jewes trumpe, untill they entred into the Kirke of North Barricke.

These confessions made the Kinge in a wonderfull admiration, and sent for the saide Geillie Duncane, who upon the like trumpe did play the saide daunce before the Kinges Majestie, who in respect of the strangeness of these matters, tooke great delight to be present at their examinations.

Item, the said Agnes Sampson confessed, that the devill, being then at North Barricke Kirke attending their coming, in the habit or likeness of a man, and seeing that they tarried over long, hee at their coming enjoined them all to a pennance, which was, that they should kiss his buttockes, in sign of duty to him; which being put over the pulpit bare, every one did as he had enjoined them: and having made his ungodly exhortations, wherein he did greatly inveigh against the Kinge of Scotland, he received their oathes for their good and true service towards him, and departed; which done, they returned to sea, and so home again.

At which time the witches demaunded of the devill why he did beare such hatred to the Kinge? Who answered, by reason the Kinge is the greatest enemie hee hath in the world.[1] All which their confessions and depositions are still extant upon record.

Item, the saide Agnes Sampson confessed before the Kinges Majestie sundrie things, which were so miraculous and strange, as that his Majestie saide they were all extreme liars; whereat shee answered, shee would not wish his Majestie to suppose her words to be false, but rather to believe them, in that shee would discover such matters unto him as his Majestie should not anie way doubt of.

And thereupon taking his Majestie a little aside, shee declared unto him the verie wordes which passed between the Kinges Majestie and his Queene at Upslo in Norway the first night of marriage, with the answere ech to other; whereat the Kinges Majestie wondered greatly, and swore by the living God, that he believed all the devills in hell could not have discovered the same, acknowledging her words to be most true, and therefore gave the more credit to the rest that is before declared.

Touching this Agnes Sampson, shee is the onlie woman who by the devill's perswasion should have intended and put in execution the Kinges Majesties death in this manner.

Shee confessed that shee tooke a blacke toade, and did hang the same up by the heeles three daies, and collected and gathered the venome it dropped and fell from it in ane oister shell, and kept the same venome close covered, untill shee should obtaine anie part or peece of foule linnen cloth that had appertained to the Kinges Majestie, as shirt, handkercher, napkin, or anie other thing, which shee practised to obtaine by meanes of one John Kers, who being attendant in his Majesties chamber, desired him for old acquaintance between them, to help her to one or a peece of such a cloth as is aforesaide, which thing the saide John Kers denyed to helpe her to, saying he coulde not helpe her unto it.

And the saide Agnes Sampson by her depositions since her apprehension, saith, that if shee had obtayned anie one peece of linnen cloth which the Kinge had worne and fowlede, shee had bewitched him to death, and put him to such extraordinarie paines, as if he had been lying upon sharp thornes and endes of needles.

Moreover shee confessed, that at the time when his Majestie was in Denmarke, shee being accompanied by the parties before speciallie named, tooke a cat and christened it, and afterwarde bounde to each part of that cat, the cheefest part of a dead man, and several joynts of his bodie; and that in the night following, the saide cat was convayed into the middest of the sea by all the witches, sayling in their riddles or cives, as is aforesaid, and so left the saide cat right before the towne of Lieth in Scotland. This doone, there did arise such a tempest in the sea, as a greater hath not beene seene; which tempest was the cause of the perishing of a boat or vessel coming over from the towne of Brunt Islande to the towne of Lieth, wherein was sundrie jewelles and rich giftes, which should have been presented to the now Queene of Scotland at her Majesties coming to Lieth.

Againe it is confessed, that the said christened cat was the cause that the Kinges Majesties shippe at his coming forth of Denmarke had a contrarie winde to the rest of his shippes then being in his companie, which thing was most strange and true as the Kinges Majestie acknowlegeth, for when the rest of the shippes had a faire and good winde, then was the winde contrarie and altogether against his Majestie; and further, the sayde witche declared, that his Majestie had never come safely from the sea, if his faith had not prevayled above their intentions.[2]

Moreover, the saide witches being demaunded how the divell would use them when he was in their companie, they confessed, that when the divel did recyeve theme for his serventes, and that they had vowed themselves unto him, then he woulde carnally use them, albeit to their little pleasure, in respect to his colde nature,[3] and would doe the like at sundrie other times.

As touching the aforesaide Doctor Fian, alias John Cunningham, the examination of his actes since his apprehension, declareth the great subteltie of the divell, and therefore maketh things to appeare the more miraculous; for being apprehended by the accusation of the saide Geillies Duncane aforesaide, who confessed he was their register, and that there was not one man suffered to come to the divel's readinges but onlie hee, the saide Doctor was taken and imprisoned, and used with the accustomed paine provided for those offences, inflicted upon the rest as is aforesaide.

First, by thrawing of his head with a rope, whereat he would confess nothing.

Secondly, hee was persuaded by faire meanes to confesse his follies, but that would prevail as little.

Lastly, hee was put to the most severe and cruell paine in the worlde, called the bootes, who, after he had received three strokes, being inquired if hee would confess his damnable actes and wicked life, his toong would not serve him to speake, in respect whereof the rest of the witches willed to search his toong, under which was found two pinnes thrust up into the heade; whereupon the witches did say, now is the charm stinted, and shewed, that those charmed pinnes were the cause he could not confess any thing: then was he immediately released of the bootes, brought before the King, his confession was taken, and his own hand willingly set thereunto, which contained as followeth:

First, that at the generall meetings of those witches, he was always present,--that he was clarke to all those that were in subjection to the divel's service, bearing the name of witches,--that always hee did take their oathes for their true service to the divel, and that he wrote for them such matters as the divel still pleased to command him.

Item, hee confessed that by his witchcraft hee did bewitch a gentleman dwelling neare to the Saltpans, where the said Doctor kept schoole, only for being enamoured of a gentlewoman whome he loved himself; by meanes of which his sorcery, witchcraft, and divelish practices, hee caused the said gentleman that once in xxiiii howers hee fell into a lunacy and madness, and so continued one whole hower together; and for the veritie of the same, he caused the gentleman to be brought before the Kinges Majestie, which was upon the xxiiii day of December last, and being in his Majesties chamber, suddenly hee gave a great scritch, and fell into madness, sometime bending himself, and sometime capering so directly up, that his heade did touch the seeling of the chamber, to the great admiration of his Majestie and others then present; so that all the gentlemen in the chamber were not able to hold him, untill they called in more helpe, who together bound him hand and foot; and suffering the said gentleman to lie still until his furie were past, hee within an hower came againe to himselfe, when being demaunded by the Kinges Majestie what he saw or did all that while, answered, that he had been in a sounde sleepe.

Item, the saide Doctor did also confesse, that hee had used meanes sundrie times to obtaine his purpose and wicked intent of the same gentlewoman, and seeing himselfe disappointed of his intention, hee determined by all wayes hee might to obtaine the same, trusting by conjuring, witchcraft, and sorcerie, to obtaine it in this manner.

It happened this gentlewoman being unmarried, had a brother who went to schoole with the saide Doctor, and calling the saide scholler to him, demaunded if hee did lie with his sister, who answered he did, by meanes whereof he thought to obtain his purpose, and therefore secretly promised to teach him without stripes, so he woulde obtaine for him three hairs of his sister's privitees, at such time as hee should spie best occasion for it; which the youth promised faithfully to performe, and vowed speedily to put it in practice, taking a piece of conjured paper of his maister to lap them in when hee had gotten them; and thereupon the boy practised nightly to obtaine his maister's purpose, especially when his sister was asleep.

But God, who knoweth the secret of all harts, and revealeth all wicked and ungodly practices, would not suffer the intents of this divelish Doctor to come to that purpose which hee supposed it woulde, and therefore to declaire that hee was heavily offended with his wicked intent, did so work by the gentlewoman's own meanes, that in the ende the same was discovered and brought to light; for shee being one night asleep, and her brother in bed with her, sodainly cried out to her mother, declaring that her brother woulde not suffer her to sleepe; whereupon, her mother having a quicke capacitie, did vehemently suspect Doctor Fian's intention, by reason shee was a witch of herselfe, and therefore presently arose, and was very inquisitive of the boy to understand his intent, and the better to know the same, did beat him with sundrie stripes, whereby hee discovered the truth unto her.

The mother, therefore, being well practised in witchcraft, did thinke it most convenient to meete with the Doctor in his owne arte, and thereupon took the paper from the boy wherein hee would have put the same haires, and went to a yong heyfer which never had borne calf, nor gone unto the bull, and with a paire of sheeres clipped off three haires from the udder of the cow, and wrapt them in the same paper, which shee again delivered to the boy, then willing him to give the same to his saide maister, which hee immediately did.

The schoole maister, so soone as he did recieve them, thinking them indeede to be the maids haires, went straight and wrought his arte upon them: But the Doctor had no sooner done his intent to them, but presently the hayfer cow, whose haires they were indeede, came unto the door of the church wherein the schoole maister was, into the which the hayfer went, and made towards the schoole maister, leaping and dancing upon him, and following him forth of the church, and to what place soever he went, to the great admiration of all the townsmen of Saltpans, and many others who did behold the same.

The report whereof made all men imagine that hee did worke it by the divel, without whome it coulde never have been so sufficiently effected; and thereupon the name of the saide Doctor Fian (who was but a young man), began to grow common among the people of Scotland, that he was secretly nominated for a notable conjurer.

All which, although in the beginning he denied, and woulde not confesse, yet having felt the paine of the bootes,[4] (and the charme stinted as aforesaide) hee confessed all the aforesaide to be most true, without producing any witnesses to justifie the same; and thereupon before the Kings Majestie hee subscribed the sayd confessione with his owne hande, which for truth remaineth upon record in Scotland.

After that the depositions and examinations of the sayd Doctor Fian, alias Cuningham, was taken, as alreddie is declared, with his own hand willingly set thereunto, hee was by the maister of the prison commited to ward, and appointed to a chamber by himselfe, where foresaking his wicked wayes, acknowledging his most ungodly life, shewing that hee had too much followed the allurements and enticements of Sathan, and fondly practised his conclusions by conjuring, witchcraft, inchantment, sorcerie, and such like, he renounced the divel and all his wicked workes, vowed to lead the lyfe of a Christian, and seemed newly converted towards God.

The morrow after, upon conference had with him, hee granted that the divel had appeared unto him in the night before, appareled all in blacke, with a white wande in his hande; and that the divel demanded of him if hee woulde continue his faithfull service, according to his first oath and promise made to that effect. Whome (as hee then saide), hee utterly renounced to his face, and said unto him in this manner, avoide, Satan, avoide, for I have listened too much unto thee, and by the same thou hast undone me, in respect whereof I utterly forsake thee: To whome the divel answered, that once ere thou die thou shalt bee mine; and with that (as hee sayd), the divel brake the white wande, and immediately vanished forth of his sight.

Thus all the daie this Doctor Fian continued verie solitarie, and seemed to have a care of his owne soule, and would call upon God, shewing himselfe penitent for his wicked lyfe; nevertheless, the same night hee found such meanes that he stole the key of the prison doore and chamber in which he was, which in the night he opened and fled awaie to the Saltpans, where he was alwayes resident, and first apprehended. Of whose sodaine departure when the Kings Majestie had intelligence, hee presently caused dilligent inquirie to be made for his apprehension; and for the better effecting thereof, hee sent public proclamations into all parts of his land to the same effect. By meanes of whose hot and harde pursuite he was again taken and brought to prison; and then being called before the Kings Highness, he was reexamined as well touching his departure, as also touching all that had before happened.

But this Doctor, notwithstanding that his owne confession appeareth remaining in recorde under his owne hande writting, and the same thereunto fixed in the presence of the Kings Majestie and sundrie of his councill, yet did he utterly denie the same.

Thereupon the Kings Majestie percieving his stubborne willfullness, concieved and imagined that in the time of his absence hee had entered into newe conference and league with the divell his maister; and that hee had beene again newly marked, for the which he was narrowly searched, but it coulde not in anie waie be founde; yet for more tryal of him to make him confesse, he was commanded to have a most strange torment, which was done in this manner following.

His nails upon all his fingers were riven and pulled off with an instrument called in Scottich a Turkas, which in England we call a payre of pincers, and under everie nayle there was thrust in thro needels over even up to the heads. At all which torments notwithstanding the Doctor never shronke anie whit, neither would he then confesse it the sooner for all the tortures inflicted upon him.

Then was hee with all convenient speede, by commandment, convaied againe to the torment of the bootes, wherein hee continued a long time, and did abide so many blows in them, that his legges were crusht and beaten together as small as might bee, and the bones and flesh so bruised, that the blood and marrow spouted forth in great abundance, whereby they were made unserviceable for ever. And notwithstanding all these grievous paines and cruel torments hee woulde not confesse anie thing, so deeply had the divel entered into his hart, that hee utterly denied that which he before avouched, and would saie nothing thereunto but this, that what hee had done and sayde before, was only done and sayde for fear of paynes which he had endured.

Upon great consideration, therefore, taken by the Kings Majestie and his councell, as well for the due execution of justice upon such detestable malefactors, as also for examples sake, to remayne a terrour to all others hereafter that shall attempt to deale in the lyke wicked and ungodlye actions, as witchcraft, sorcerie, cunjuration, and such lyke, the saide Doctor Fian was soon after arraigned, condemned, and adjudged by the law to die, and then to be burned according to the lawe of that lande provided in that behalfe. Whereupon he was put into a carte, and being first stranguled, hee was immediately put into a great fire, being readie provided for that purpose, and there burned in the Castile Hill of Edenbrough, on a Saterdaie in the ende of Januarie last past, 1591.

The rest of the witches which are not yet executed, remayne in prison till farther triall and knowledge of his Majesties pleasure.

***

This strange discourse before recited, may perhaps give some occasion of doubt to such as shall happen to reade the same, and thereby conjecture that the Kings Majestie would hazzarde himselfe in the presence of such notorious witches, least thereby might have ensued great danger to his person and the general state of the land, which thing in truth might wel have beene feared. But to answer generally to such let this suffice; that first it is well known that the King is the child and servant of God, and they but the servants to the devil; he is the Lord's anointed, and they but vesseles of God's wrath; hee is a true Christian, and trusteth in God; they worse than infidels, for they only trust in the divel, who daily serve them, till hee have brought them to utter destruction. But hereby it seemeth that his Highness carried a magnanimous and undaunted mind, not feared with their inchantments, but resolute in this, that so long as God is with him hee feareth not who is against him; and trulie, the whole scope of this Treatise dooth so plainlie laie open the wonderfull Providence of the Almightie, that if hee had not beene defended by his omnipotence and power, his Highness had never returned alive in his voiage from Denmarke, so there is no doubt but God woulde as well defend him on the land as on the sea, where they pretended their damnable practice.

FINIS.

Footnotes:

1. James, who boasted that he was born in 'the purest church on earth,' and whose courtiers called him 'the Childe of God,' was no doubt highly gratified at this declaration of the devil's hatred, 'because he was his greatest enemie on earth.' This was such a piece of flattery as suited the meridian of the monarch's intellects. ED.

2. It no doubt required the penetration of a witch to discover the strength of James's faith, which prevailed against their incantations, and saved him from perishing at sea. Those who conducted the

examination of the witches, no doubt knew well enough how to extract this little piece of delicate flattery from the hags, so gratifying to the palate of their master. ED.

3. In the records of the kirk-session of Torryburn, in Fifeshire, so late as 1703, is the confession of one Lillias Eddie, a supposed witch, who immediately after she had been initiated in the infernal mysteries, was taken behind a stook, it (being harvest time), and carressed by the devil. She likewise complains that his embraces were cold and unsatisfactory. The gross indelicacy of such stories are only to be equalled by their absurdity. What a picture does it present to readers of the present day, of the manners of that age, when such topics could be gravely discussed by the King in councill!!

4. We have no doubt that the bootes were a most efficacious engine to procure a confession, and the Doctor would most likely have confessed that he had the moon in his pocket by the same means. ED.

Another Account of the Foregoing Transactions, Extracted from Sir James Melvil's Memoirs, page 388, octavo edition.

About this time many witches were taken in Lothian, who deposed concerning some design of the Earl of Bothwell's against his Majesty's person. Which coming to the said Earl's ears, he entered in ward within the Castle of Edinburgh, desiring to be tried, alledging that the devil, who was a liar from the beginning, ought not to be credited, nor yet the witches, his sworn servants. Especially a renowned midwife called Amy Simson affirmed, that she, in company with nine other witches, being convened in the night beside Prestonpans, the devil their master being present, standing in the midst of them, a body of wax, shapen and made by the said Amy Simson, wrapped within a linnen cloth, was first delivered to the devil; who, after he had pronounced his verdict, delivered the said picture to Amy Simson, and she to her next neighbour, and so every one round about, saying, This is King James VI. ordered to be consumed at the instance of a nobleman, Francis Earl Bothwell. Afterward again at their meeting by night in the kirk of North Berwick, where the devil, clad in a black gown, with a black hat upon his head, preached unto a great number of them out of the pulpit, having light candles round about him.

The effect of his language was to know what hurt they had done; how many they had gained to their opinion since the last meeting; what success the melting of the picture had, and such other vain things. And because an old silly poor ploughman, called Gray Meilt, chanced to say, that nothing ailed the King yet, God be thanked, the devil gave him a great blow. Thus divers among them entred in reasoning, marvelling that all their devilry could do no harm to the King, as it had done to divers others. The devil answered, il est un homme de Dieu, certainly he is a man of God, and does no wrong wittingly, but he is inclined to all Godliness, justice, and vertue, therefore God hath preserved him in the midst of many dangers.[5] Now, after that the devil had ended his admonitions, he came down out of the pulpit, and caused all the company come kiss his arse; which they said was cold like ice, his body hard like iron, as they thought who handled him, his face was terrible, his nose like the beak of an eagle, great burning eyes, his hands and his legs were hoary, with claws upon his hands and feet like the griffin;--he spoke with a low voice.

The tricks and tragedies he played then among so many men and women in this country, will hardly get credit by posterity; the history whereof, with their whole depositions, was written by Mr James Carmichael, minister of Haddington.[6] Among other things, some of them did shew, that there was a westland man, called Richard Graham, who had a familiar spirit, the which Richard they said could both do and tell many things, chiefly against the Earl of Bothwell. Whereupon the said Richard Graham was apprehended and brought to Edinburgh; and, being examined before his Majesty, I being present, he granted that he had a familiar spirit which shewed him sundrie things, but he denied that he was a witch, or had any frequentation with them. But when it was answered again, how that Amy Simson had declared, that he caused the Earl of Bothwell address him to her, he granted that to be true, and that the Earl of Bothwell had knowledge of him by Effe Machalloun and Barbary Napier, Edinburgh women. Whereupon he was sent for by the Earl Bothwell, who required his help to cause the Kings Majesty his master to like well of him. And to that effect he gave the said Earl some drug or herb, willing him at some convenient time to touch therewith his Majesty's face. Which being done by the said Earl ineffectually, he dealt again with the said Richard to get his Majesty wrecked, as Richard alledged; who said, he could not do such things himself, but that a notable midwife, who was a witch, called Amy Simson, could bring any such purpose to pass. Thus far the said Richard Graham affirmed divers times before the council; nevertheless, he was burnt with the said Simson, and many other witches. This Richard alledged, that it was certain what is reported of the fairies, and that spirits may take a form, and be seen, though not felt.

Footnotes:

5. It was certainly very kind in the devil thus to vouch for James's being 'a man of God, and one who did no wrong wittingly, but was inclined to all Godliness, Justice, and Virtue.' This is a most excellent character. But posterity are inclined to be of Earl Bothwell's opinion, that the devil is a liar, and ought not to be credited. ED.

6. This probably is the author of the foregoing 'True Discourse.' ED.

Advertisement

From the foregoing 'True Discourse,' it will be seen what an active part James took in the examination of Doctor Fian and the other witches. From this source he most probably collected those materials which he has wrought up into a Daemonologie, a work which no doubt contributed to obtain for him from the English bishops, the appelation of 'the British Solomon.' In this work he appears to be more intimately acquainted with the internal polity of the Devil's kingdom, than he was with his own. The kingdom of Sathan was then in its zenith of power; but, like other states and kingdoms, it has sunk into great weakness and debility. The 'horn'd diel,' who could then make the greatest personages shake in their shoes, cannot now frighten a child; and the 'roaring lion,' who used to be going about seeking whom he might devour, must surely be a better housekeeper than formerly, as he is never seen abroad, even by an old woman.

From the Daemonologie we have made copious extracts, that our readers may have an idea of the days of 'langsyne,' when there was plenty of diels, witches, fairies, and water kelpies, all over the country. Those, therefore, who are anxious to know how affairs are managed in the 'kingdom of darkness,' and can rely on the word of a king for the truth of it, will be here amply gratified.

So, courteous reader, I bid thee farewell,

The EDITOR.

Part III

Extracts From King James's Daemonologie, Concerning Sorcery and Witchcraft

The First Entresse and Prentiship of them that give themselves to Witchcraft.

The persons that give themselves to witchcraft, are of two sorts, rich and of better accompt, poore and of baser degree. These two degrees answere to the passions in them, which the divell uses as meanes to entice them to his service; for such of them as are in great miserie and povertie, he allures to follow him, by promising unto them great riches and worldly commoditie. Such as though rich, yet burne in a desperate desire of revenge, he allures them by promises to get their turne satisfied to their hearts contentment. It is to be noted now, that that olde and craftie enemie of ours assailes none, though touched with any of these two extremities, except he first finde an entresse ready for him, either by the great ignorance of the person he dealeth with, joyned with an evill life, or else by their carelessnesse and contempt of God. And finding them in an utter despaire, he prepares the way by feeding them craftely in their humour, and filling them further and further with despaire, while hee finde the time proper to discover himself unto them. At which time, either upon their walking solitarie in the fieldes, or else lying pausing in their bed, but alwaies without the company of any other, hee, either by a voyce, or in likenesse of a man, inquires of them what troubles them, and promiseth them a suddaine and certaine way of remedie, upon condition, on the other part, that they follow his advise, and doe such things as he will require of them. Their mindes being prepared beforehand, they easily agree unto that demand of his, and syne sets another tryist where they may meete againe. At which time, before hee proceede any further with them, hee first perswades them to addict themselves to his service, which being easily obtained, he then discovers what he is unto them, makes them to renounce their God and baptisme directly, and gives them his marke upon some secret place of their bodie, which remaines soare unhealed while his next meeting with them, and thereafter ever insensible, howsoever it be nipped or pricked by any, as is daily prooved, to give them a proofe thereby, that as in that doing he could hurt and heale them, so all their ill and well doing thereafter must depend upon him; and, besides that, the intolerable dolour that they feele in that place where he hath marked them, serves to waken them, and not to let them rest, while their next meeting againe; fearing lest otherwaies they might either forget him, being as new prentises, and not well enough founded yet in that fiendly follie; or else remembering of that horrible promise they made him at their last meeting, they might skunner at the same, and presse to call it backe. At their third meetinge, hee makes a shew to be carefull to performe his promises, either by teaching them waies how to get themselves revenged, if they be of that sort, or else by teaching them lessons how by most vile and unlawfull meanes they may obtaine gaine and worldly commoditie, if they be of the other sort.

***

The Witches actions divided into two parts--The actions proper to their own persons--The forme of their Conventions and adoring of their Master.

Their actions may be divided into two parts; the actions of their owne persons, and the actions proceeding from them towards any other; and this division being well understood, will easily resolve what is possible to them to doe. For although all that they confesse is no lie upon their part, yet doubtlesly, in my opinion, a part of it is not indeede according as they take it to be, for the divell illudes the senses of these schollers of his in many things.

To the effect that they may performe such services of their false master as he employs them in, the devill, as God's ape, counterfeits in his servants this service and forme of adoration that God prescribed and made his servants to practise; for as the servants of God publikely use to conveene for serving of him, so makes he them in great numbers to conveene (though publikely they dare not), for his service. As none conveenes to the adoration and worshipping of God, except they be marked with his seale, the sacrament of baptisme; so none serves Satan, and conveenes to the adoring of him, that are not marked with that marke whereof I alreadie spake. As the minister sent by God teacheth plainely at the time of their publike conventions, how to serve him in spirit and trewth, so that unclean spirit, in his owne person, teacheth his disciples at the time of their conveening, how to worke all kind of mischiefe, and craves coumpt of all their horrible and detestable proceedings passed for advancement of his service: Yea, that hee may the more vilely counterfeit and scorne God, he oft times makes his slaves to conveene in these very places which are destinate and ordained for the conveening of the servants of God, (I meane by churches.) But this farre which I have yet said, I not onely take it to be trew in their opinions, but even so to be indeed; for the forme that he used in counterfeiting God amongst the Gentiles, makes me so to think; as God spake by his oracles, spake he not so by his? As God had as well bloodie sacrifices, as others without blood, had not he the like? As God had churches sanctified to his service, with altars, priests, sacrifices, ceremonies, and prayers, had he not the like polluted to his service? As God gave responses by Urim and Thummim, gave he not his responses by the intralles of beasts, by the singing of fowles, and by their actions in the aire? As God by visions, dreames, and extasies, revealed what was to come, and what was his will unto his servants, used hee not the like meanes to forewarne his slaves of things to come? Yea, even as God loved cleanenesse, hated vice and impuritie, and appointed punishments therefore, used he not the like, (though falsly I grant, and but in eschewing the lesse inconvenience, to draw them upon a greater), yet dissimulated he not, I say, so farre as to appoint his priests to keepe their bodies cleane and undefiled, before their asking responses of him? And fained he not God, to be a protectour of every vertue, and a just revenger of the contrarie? This reason then mooves me, that as he is that same divell, and as crafty now as he was then, so will he not spare as pertly in these actions that I have spoken of concerning the witches' persons; but further, witches oft times confesse, not only his conveening in the church with them, but his occupying of the pulpit: Yea, their forme of adoration to be the kissing of his hinder parts, which, though it seeme ridiculous, yet may it likewise be trew, seeing we reade that in Calicute he appeared in forme of a goat-bucke, hath publikely that unhonest homage done unto him by every one of the people. So ambitious is he, and greedy of honour, (which procured his fall) that he will even imitate God in that part where it is said, that Moyses could see but the hinder parts of God for the brightnesse of his glory.

***

What are the wayes possible whereby the Witches may transport themselves to places farre distant?--And what are impossible and meere illusions of Satan?

PHI.--But by what way say they, or thinke yee it possible, they can come to these unlawfull conventions?[7]

EPI.--There is the thing which I esteeme their senses to be deluded in, and though they lie not in confessing of it, because they thinke it to be trew, yet not to be so in substance or effect; for they say, that by divers meanes they may conveene, either to the adoring of their master, or to the putting in practise any service of his committed unto their charge; one way is naturall, which is naturall riding, going, or sailing, at what houre their master comes and advertises them; and this way may be easily beleeved; another way is somewhat more strange, and yet it is possible to bee trew, which is, by being caried by the force of the spirit, which is their conducter, either above the earth, or above the sea, swiftly to the place where they are to meet; which I am perswaded to bee likewise possible, in respect, that as Habakkuk was carried by the angel in that forme to the den where Daniel lay, so I thinke the divell will be readie to imitate God as well in that as in other things; which is much more possible to him to doe, being a spirit, then to a mighty wind, being but a naturall meteore to transport from one place to another a solide body, as is commonly and daily seene in practise; but in this violent forme they cannot be caried but a short bounds, agreeing with the space that they may retain their breath, for if it were longer, their breath could not remain unextinguished, their body being caried in such a violent and forcible manner; as by example, if one fall off a small height, his life is but in perill, according to the hard or soft lighting; but if one fall from an high and stay rocke, his breath will be forcibly banished from the body before he can win to the earth, as is oft seene by experience; and in this transporting they say themselves, that they are invisible to any other, except amongst themselves, which may also be possible in my opinion; for if the devill may forme what kinde of impressions he pleases in the aire, why may he not farre easilier thicken and obscure so the aire that is next about them, by contracting it straite together, that the beames of any other man's eyes cannot pierce throw the same to see them? But the third way of their comming to their conventions is that wherein I thinke them deluded; for some of them say, that being transformed in the likenesse of a little beast or foule, they will come and pierce through whatsoever house or church, though all ordinarie passages be closed, by whatsoever open the aire may enter in at; and some say, that their bodies lying still, as in an extasie, their spirits will be ravished out of their bodies, and caried to such places; and for verifying thereof, will give evident tokens, as well by witnesses that have seene their body lying senseless in the mean time, as by naming persons with whom they met, and giving tokens what purpose was amongst them, whom otherwise they could not have known; for this forme of journeying they affirme to use most, when they are transported from one countrey to another.

PHI.--But the reasons that moove me to thinke that these are meere illusions, are these--first, for them that are transformed in likenesse of beasts or foules, can enter through so narrow passages, although I may easily beleeve that the divell could by his workmanship upon the aire, make them appeare to be in such formes, either to themselves, or to others; yet how can he contract a solide body within so little room? I think it is directly contrary to itselfe; for to be made so little, and yet not diminished; to be so straitly drawn together, and yet feele no paine, I thinke it is so contrary to the qualitie of a naturall bodie, and so like to the little transubstantiate god in the Papists masse, that I can never beleeve it. So to have a quantitie, is so proper to a solide body, that as all philosophers conclude, it cannot be any more without one, then a spirit can have one; for when Peter came out of the prison, and the doores all locked, it was not by any contracting of his body in so little roome, but by the giving place of the doore, though unespied by the gaylors; and yet is there no comparison, when this is done, betwixt the power of God and of the divel. As to their forme of extasie and spirituall transporting, it is certaine the soules going out of the body, is the onely definition of naturall death; and who are once dead, God forbid we should thinke that it should lie in the power of all the divels in hell to restore them to their life again, although he can put his owne spirit in a dead body, for that is the office properly belonging to God; and, besides that, the soule once parting from the body, cannot wander any longer in the world, but to the owne resting place must it goe immediately, abiding the conjunction of the body again at the latter day. And what Christ or the prophets did miraculously in this case, it can in no Christian man's opinion be made common with the divel. As for any tokens that they give for proving of this, it is very possible to the divel's craft to perswade them to these meanes; for he being a spirit, may he not so ravish their thoughts, and dull their senses, that their body lying as dead, he may object to their spirits, as it were in a dreame, and represent such formes of persons, of places, and other circumstances, as he pleases to illude them with? Yea, that he may deceive them with the greater efficacie, may he not, at the same instant, by fellow angels of his, illude such other persons so in that same fashion, with whom hee makes them to beleeve that they mette, that all their reports and tokens, though severally examined, may every one agree with another? And that whatsoever actions, either in hurting men or beasts, or whatsoever other thing that they falsly imagine at that time to have done, may by himselfe or his marrowes at that same time be done indeed; so as if they would give for a token of their being ravished at the death of such a person within so short a space thereafter, whom they beleeve to have poisoned or witched at that instant, might he not at that same houre have smitten that same person, by the permission of God, to the farther deceiving of them, and to moove others to beleeve them? And this is surely the likelyest way, and most according to reason, which my judgement can finde out in this and whatsoever other unnatural points of their confession.

***

Witches actions towards others--Why there are more Women of that Craft then Men--What things are possible to them to effectuate by the power of their Master--What is the surest remedy of the harmes done by them.

PHI.--FORSOOTH your opinion in this seems to cary most reason with it; and since ye have ended then the actions belonging properly to their owne persons, say forward now to their actions used towards others.

EPI.--In their actions used towards others, three things ought to be considered; first, the manner of their consulting thereupon; next, their part as instruments; and, last, their master's part, who puts the same in execution. As to their consultations thereupon, they use them oftest in the churches, where they conveene for adoring; at which time their master enquiring at them what they would be at, every one of them propones unto him what wicked turne they would have done, either for obtaining of riches, or for revenging them upon any whom they have malice at; who granting their demaund, as no doubt willingly he will, since it is to doe evill, hee teacheth them the meanes whereby they may doe the same. As for little trifling turnes that women have adoe with, he causeth them to joynt dead corpses, and to make powders thereof, mixing such other things thereamongst as he gives unto them.

PHI.--But before ye goe further, permit me, I pray you, to interrupt you one word, which ye have put me in memorie of by speaking of women; What can be the cause that there are twentie women given to that craft where there is one man?

EPI.--The reason is easie, for as that sexe is frailer than man is, so is it easier to be intrapped in these grosse snares of the divell, as was over-well prooved to be trew, by the serpent's deceiving of Eve at the beginning, which makes him the homelier with that sexe sensine.

PHI.--Returne now where ye left.

EPI.--To some others at these times he teacheth how to make pictures of waxe or clay, that by the roasting thereof, the persons that they beare the name of may be continually melted or dried away by continuall sicknesse. To some he gives such stones or pouders as will helpe to cure or cast on diseases; and to some hee teacheth kindes of uncouth poysons, which mediciners understand not; not that any of these meanes which he teacheth them (except the poysons, which are composed of things naturall), can of themselves helpe any thing to these turnes that they are employed in, but onely being God's ape, as well in that, as in all other things. Even as God by his sacraments, which are earthly of themselves, workes a heavenly effect, though no waves by any cooperation in them; and as Christ by clay and spettle wrought together, opened the eyes of the blinde man, suppose there was no vertue in that which he outwardly applied, so the divel will have his outward meanes to be shewes as it were of his doing, which hath no part or cooperation in his turnes with him, how farre that ever the ignorants be abused in the contrarie. And as to the effects of these two former parts, TO WIT, the consultations and the outward meanes, they are so wonderfull, as I dare not alledge any of them without joyning a sufficient reason of the possibilitie thereof; for leaving all the small trifles among wives, and to speake of the principall points of their craft, for the common trifles thereof, they can doe without converting well enough by themselves, these principall points, I say, are these--they can make men or women to love or hate other, which may be very possible to the divel to effectuate, seeing he being a subtile spirit, knowes well enough how to perswade the corrupted affection of them whom God will permit him to deal with,-- they can lay the sicknesse of one upon another, which likewise is very possible unto him; for since by God's permission he laide sicknesse upon Job, why may he not farre easilier lay it upon any other? For as an old practitian, hee knowes well enough what humour domines most in any of us, and as a spirit he can subtillie waken up the same, making it peccant, or to abound, as hee thinkes meet, for troubling of us, when God will so permit him. And for the taking off of it, no doubt he will be glad to relieve such of present paine as he may thinke by these meanes to perswade to be catched in his everlasting snares and fetters. They can bewitch and take the life of men or women, by roasting of the pictures, as I spake of before, which likewise is verie possible to their master to performe; for although that instrument of waxe have no vertue in that turne doing, yet may he not very well, even by the same measure that his conjured slaves melts that waxe at the fire, may he not, I say, at these same times, subtily as a spirit, so weaken and scatter the spirits of life of the patient, as may make him on the one part, for faintnesse, to sweat out the humour of his bodie, and on the other part, for the not concurrence of these spirits, which causes his digestion, so debilitate his stomacke, that this humour radicall continually, sweating out on the one part, and no new good sucke being put in the place thereof, for lacke of digestion on the other, he at last shall vanish away, even as his picture will doe at the fire? And that knavish and cunning workeman, by troubling him onely at sometimes, makes a proportion so neere betwixt the working of the one and the other, that both shall end as it were at one time. They can raise stormes and tempests in the aire, either upon sea or land, though not universally, but in such a particular place and prescribed bounds, as God will permit them so to trouble. Which likewise is very easy to be discerned from any other naturall tempests that are meteores, in respect of the sudden and violent raising thereof, together with the short induring of the same. And this is likewise very possible to their master to doe, hee having such affinitie with the aire, as being a spirit, and having such power of the forming and mooving thereof; for in the Scripture, that stile of the prince of the aire, is given unto him. They can make folkes to become phrenticque or maniacque, which likewise is very possible to their master to doe, since they are but naturall sicknesses, and so he may lay on these kindes as well as any others. They can make spirits either to follow and trouble persons, or haunt certaine houses, and affray oftentimes the inhabitants, as hath been knowne to be done by our witches at this time. And likewise, they can make some to bee possessed with spirits, and so to become very demoniacques; and this last sort is very possible likewise to the divel their master to doe, since he may easily send his owne angels to trouble in what forme he pleases any whom God will permit him so to use.

PHI.--But will God permit these wicked instruments, by the power of the devill their master, to trouble by any of these meanes any that beleeve in him?

EPI.--No doubt, for there are three kindes of folkes whom God will permit so to be tempted or troubled; the wicked for their horrible sinnes, to punish them in the like measure; the godly that are sleeping in any great sinnes or infirmities, and weaknesse in faith, to waken them up the faster by such an uncouth forme; and even some of the best, that their patience may be tried before the world, as Job's was. For why may not God use any kinde of extraordinarie punishment, when it pleases him, as well as the ordinarie rods of sicknesse or other adversities?

PHI.--Who then may be free from these devilish practises?

EPI.--No man ought to presume so farre as to promise any impunitie to himselfe; for God hath before all beginnings, preordinated as well the particular sorts of plagues, as of benefites, for every man, which in the owne time he ordaines them to be visited with; and yet ought we not to be the more afraide for that, of any thing that the divell and his wicked instruments can doe against us, for we daily fight against the divell in a hundreth other wayes; and therefore, as a valiant captaine affraies no more being at the combate, nor stayes from his purpose for the rummishing shot of a canon, nor the small clacke of a pistolet, suppose he be not certaine what may light upon him; even so ought we boldly to goe forward in fighting against the divell, without any great terrour for these his rarest weapons, nor for the ordinary, whereof we have daily the proofe.

PHI.--Is it not lawfull then, by the helpe of some other witch, to cure the disease that is casten on by that craft?

EPI.--No wayes lawfull, for it is an axiome of theologie, that we are not to doe evil, that good maie come of it.

PHI.--How then may these diseases be lawfully cured?

EPI.--Only by earnest prayer unto God, by amendment of their lives, and by sharpe pursuing every one, according to his calling of these instruments of Satan, whose punishment to the death will be a salutarie sacrifice for the patient. And this is not onely the lawfull way, but likewise the most sure; for by the devil's meanes can never the devill be casten out, as Christ sayth; and when such a cure is used, it may well serve for a short time, but at the last it will doubtlesly tend to the utter perdition of the patient, both in body and soule.

What sort of Folkes are least or most subject to receive harme by Witchcraft--What power they have to harme the Magistrate, and upon what respects they have any power in prison--And to what end may or will the Devill appeare to them therein--Upon what respects the Devill appeares in sundry shapes to sundry of them at any time.

PHI.--But who dare take upon him to punish them, if no man can be sure to be free from their unnatural invasions?

EPI.--Wee ought not the more of that restraine from vertue, that the way whereby we clime thereunto be straight and perillous; but, besides that, as there is no kinde of persons so subject to receive harme of them, as these that are of infirme and weake faith, so have they so small power over none, as over such as zealously and earnestly pursue them.

PHI.--Then they are like the pest which smites these sickarest that flies it farthest?

EPI.--It is even so with them, for neither is it able to them to use any false cure upon a patient, except the patient first beleeve in their power, and so hazard the tinsell of his owne soule, nor yet can they have lesse power to hurt any, nor such as contemne most their doings, so being it comes of faith, and not of any vaine arrogancie in themselves.

PHI.--But what is their power against the Magistrate?

EPI.--Lesse or greater, according as he deales with them; for if hee be slothfull towards them, God is very able to make them instruments to waken and punish his sloth; but if he be the contrary, hee, according to the just law of God, and allowable law of all nations, will be diligent in examining and punishing of them, God will not permit their master to trouble or hinder so good a worke.

PHI.--But fra they be once in hands and firmance, have they any further power in their craft?

EPI.--That is according to the forme of their detention; if they be but apprehended and deteined by any private person, upon other private respects, their power no doubt, either in escaping, or in doing hurt, is no lesse nor ever it was before; but if, on the other part, their apprehending and detention be by the lawfull magistrate, upon the just respects of their guiltinesse in that craft, their power is then no greater than before that ever they medled with their master; for where God begins justly to strike by his lawfull lieutenants, it is not in the devil's power to defraud or bereave him of the office, or effect of his powerful and revenging scepter.

PHI.--But will never their master come to visite them fra they be once apprehended and put in firmance?

EPI.--That is according to the estate that these miserable wretches are in, for if they be obstinate in still denying, he will not spare, when hee findes time to speake with them, either if he finde them in any comfort, to fill them more and more with the vaine hope of some manner of reliefe, or else if he finde them in a deepe despaire, by all meanes to augment the same, and to perswade them by some extraordinarie meanes to put themselves downe, which very commonly they doe; but if they be penitent and confesse, God will not permit him to trouble them any more with his presence and allurements.

PHI.--It is not good using his counsell I see then; but I would earnestly know, when he appeares to them in prison, what formes uses he then to take?

EPI.--Divers formes, even as hee uses to doe at other times unto them; but ordinarily in such a forme as they agree upon among themselves; or, if they be but prentises, according to the qualitie of their circles or conjurations: yet to these capped creatures he appeares as he pleases, and as he findes meetest for their humours; for even at their publicke conventions, hee appeares to divers of them in divers formes, as we have found by the difference of their confessions in that point; for he deluding them with vaine impressions in the aire, makes himselfe to seeme more terrible to the grosser sort, that they may thereby be mooved to feare and reverence him the more, and lesse monstrous and uncouth like againe to the craftier sort, lest otherwise they might sturre and skunner at his uglinesse.

PHI.--How can he then be felt, as they confesse they have done, if his body be but of aire?

EPI.--I heare little of that amongst their confessions, yet may he make himselfe palpable, either by assuming any dead bodie, and using the ministerie thereof, or else by deluding as well their sense of feeling as seeing, which is not impossible to him to doe, since all our senses, as wee are so weake, and even by ordinarie sicknesses, will be oftentimes deluded.

PHI.--But I would speere one word further yet concerning his appearing to them in prison, which is this, may any other that chances to be present at that time in the prison see him as well as they?

EPI.--Sometimes they will, and sometimes not, as it pleases God.

Of the Tryall and Punishment of Witches--What sort of Accusation ought to be admitted against them--What is the cause of the increasing so farre of their number in this age.

PHI.--Then to make an end of our conference, since I see it drawes late, what forme of punishment thinke yee merit these witches?

EPI.--They ought to be put to death according to the law of God, the civill and imperial law, and municipall law of all Christian nations.

PHI.--But what kinde of death I pray you?

EPI.--It is commonly used by fire, but that is an indifferent thing to be used in every countrey, according to the law or custome thereof.

PHI.--But ought no sexe, age, nor ranke, to be exempted?

EPI.--None at all, (being so used by the lawfull magistrate), for it is the highest point of idolatry wherein no exception is admitted by the law of God.

PHI.--Then barnes may not be spared?

EPI.--Yea, not a haire the lesse of my conclusion, for they are not that capable of reason as to practise such things; and for any being in company, and not reveiling thereof, their less and ignorant age will no doubt excuse them.

PHI.--I see ye condemne them all that are of the counsell of such craftes.

EPI.--No doubt the consulters, trusters in, overseers, interteiners, or stirrers up of these craftes folkes, are equally guiltie with themselves that are the practisers.

PHI.--Whether may the prince then, or supreme magistrate, spare or oversee any that are guilty of that craft, upon some great respects knowen to him?

EPI.--The prince or magistrate, for further trials cause, may continue the punishing of them such a certaine space as he thinkes convenient, but in the end to spare the life, and not to strike when God bids strike, and so severely punish in so odious a fault and treason against God, it is not onely unlawfull, but doubtlesse no lesse sinne in that magistrate, nor it was in Saules sparing of Agag; and so comparable to the sinne of witchcraft itselfe, as Samuel alledged at that time.

PHI.--Surely then, I think since this crime ought to be so severely punished, judges ought to beware to condemne any but such as they are sure are guiltie, neither should the clattering report of a carling serve in so weightie a case.

EPI.--Judges ought indeede to beware whom they condemne, for it is as great a crime (as Solomon saith), to condemne the innocent as to let the guilty escape free, neither ought the report of any one infamous person be admitted for a sufficient proof which can stand of no law.

PHI.--And what may a number of guilty persons confessions worke against one that is accused?

EPI.--The assise must serve for interpretour of our law in that respect, but in my opinion, since in a matter of treason against the prince, barnes or wives, or never so diffamed persons, may of our law serve for sufficient witnesses and proofes, I thinke surely that by a farre greater reason such witnesses may be sufficient in matters of high treason against God; for who but witches can be prooves, and so witnesses of the doings of witches?

PHI.--Indeed, I trow they will be loath to put any honest man upon their counsell; but what if they accuse folke to have been present at their imaginar conventions in the spirit, when their bodies lye senseless, as ye have said?

EPI.--I thinke they are not a haire the less guiltie; for the divell durst never have borrowed their shadow or similitude to that turne, if their consent had not beene at it; and the consent in these turnes is death of the lawe.

PHI.--Then Samuel was a witch, for the divell resembled his shape, and played his person in giving response to Saul.

EPI.--Samuel was dead as well before that, and so none could slaunder him with medling in that unlawful arte; for the cause why, as I take it, that God will not permit Satan to use the shapes of similitudes of any innocent persons at such unlawfull times is, that God will not permit that any innocent persons shall be slandered with that vile defection, for then the divell would finde waies anew to calumniate the best; and this we have in proofe by them that are carried with the pharie, who never see the shadowes of any in that court but of them that thereafter are tryed to have beene brethren and sisters of that craft. And this was likewise proved by the confession of a young lasse troubled with spirits, laid on her by witchcraft; that although she saw the shapes of divers men and women troubling her, and naming the persons whom these shadowes represent; yet never one of them are founde to be innocent, but all clearely tryed to be most guiltie, and the most part of them confessing the same. And, besides that, I thinke it hath beene seldome heard tell of, that any whom persons guiltie of that crime accused, as having knowen them to be their marrows by eye-sight, and not by hearesay, but such as were so accused of witchcraft, could not be clearly tried upon them, were at the least publikely knowen to be of a very evill life and reputation; so jealous is God of the fame of them that are innocent in such causes. And, besides that, there are two other good helps that may be used for their triall; the one is, the finding of their marke, and the trying the insensibleness thereof; the other is their fleeting on the water, for as in a secret murther, if the dead carkasse be at any time thereafter handled by the murtherer, it will gush out of bloud, as if the bloud were crying to the heaven for revenge of the murtherer, God having appointed that secret supernaturall signe for triall of that secret unnatural crime, so it appeares that God hath appointed (for a supernatural signe of the monstrous impietie of witches), that the water shall refuse to receive them in her bosome that have shaken off them the sacred water of baptisme, and wilfully refused the benefitie thereof. No, not so much as their eyes are able to shed teares (threaten and torture them as ye please), while first they repent, (God not permitting them to dissemble their obstinacie in so horrible a crime) albeit the women kind especially, be able otherwayes to shed teares at every light occasion when they will, yea, although it were dissemblingly like the crocodiles.

PHI.--Well, wee have made this conference to last as long as leisure would permit; and to conclude then, since I am to take my leave of you, I pray God to purge this countrey of these divellish practises, for they were never so rife in these parts as they are now.

EPI.--I pray God that so be too; but the causes are over manifest that make them to be so rife; for the great wickedness of the people on the one hand, procures this horrible defection, whereby God justly punisheth sinne by a greater iniquitie; and on the other part, the consummation of the world and our deliverance drawing neere, makes Satan to rage the more in his instruments, knowing his kingdome to be so neere an end.--And so farewell for this time.

THE END

Footnotes:

7. The Daemonologie is written by way of dialogue, in which Philomathes and Epistemon reason the matter.

Part IV

An Answer of a Letter from A Gentleman in Fife, to a Nobleman, Containting a Brief Account of the Barbarous and Illegal Treatment These Poor Women Accused of Witchcraft Met with from the Bailles of Pittenweem and Others--with some Observations Thereon.

To which is added, An Account of the Horrid and Barbarous Murder, in a Letter from a Gentleman in Fife to his Friend in Edinburgh, February 5th, 1705.

Printed in the Year 1705.

The two following Tracts give an account of the witches of Pittenweem in 1705. The first is a concise relation of facts, in which the minister and magistrates are placed in no very favourable point of view. The second is an answer to the first, and seems chiefly intended to obviate the charges that are preferred against the minister and baillies, but in our opinion with no great success, as the principal facts are admitted, and the only defence set up is, that the women were in reality witches. We have given this author's story in his own words, with such of his remarks as bear upon the narrative of the other pamphlet, which is all that is necessary at the present day.

EDITOR.

An Answer of a Letter from a Gentlemen in Fife, &c.

My Lord,

I reckon myself very much honoured by your Lordship's letter, desiring me to write you an account of that horrible murder committed in Pittenweem. I doubt not, but by this time, your Lordship has seen the gentleman's letter to his friend thereanent; I refer you to it, the author thereof being so well informed, and so ingenous, that I'll assure you, there is nothing in it but what is generally talked and believed to be true.

All I can contribute to your Lordship's further information, shall be by way of a brief narrative of the minister and baillies unwarrantable imprisoning, and barbarous treating of the poor women.

I need not write your Lordship a character of Patrick Morton, being now sufficiently known for a cheat.

It was upon his accusation allennarly the minister and baillies imprisoned these poor women, and set a guard of drunken fellows about them, who by pinching and pricking some of them with pins and elsions, kept them from sleep for several days and nights together, the marks whereof were seen by severals a month thereafter. This cruel usage made some of them learn to be so wise as acknowledge every question that was asked them; whereby they found the minister and baillies well pleased, and themselves better treated.

Notwithstanding of all this, some of the more foolish continued, as the minister said, hardened in the devil's service, such as White, Jack, Wallace, Patrick, and others; all which, save the first, were ordered to the stocks, where they lay for several weeks.

All this while Patrick Morton's melancholly fancy (to give it no harsher term), being too much encouraged by severals, and particularly by the minister's reading to him the case of Barrgarran's daughter, continued roving after a wonderful manner, accusing for his tormentors some of the most considerable mens' wives in the town, but such as the minister and baillies durst not venture to imprison.--By this your Lordship may see, it was only the weakest that went to the walls.

My Lord Rothes, accompanied with several gentlemen of good sense and reputation, came to Pittenweem, where finding these poor womens' confessions no wise satisfying, and Patrick Morton a cheat, informed the privy council thereof, who sent an order to send Patrick over to them. This turn being given, and Patrick finding that things were not likely to go so favourably with him as he before fancied, began to draw to his breeches, and in a short time recovered his former health, in which he still continues. By this time the baillies began to be as earnest in emptying their prisons, as ever they were forward in filling them; so after a long and serious deliberation, they set them at liberty: but that their last step might be as illegal as their first, obliged each of them to pay the town-officer the sum of 8 lib. Scots; to pay which, some of them were forced to sell some linnen they had reserved for their dead shirts and wynding sheets.

I beg your Lordship's further patience a little to read these few following observations: Obs. 1st, The baillies and minister sent and brought several of these women from places without their jurisdiction--one from Anstruther, and another from the country at six miles distance.

Obs. 2d, What good could the minister propose to Patrick Morton by reading to him the book intituled the case of Barrgarran's daughter?

Obs. 3d, After so much injustice done to these poor women, the baillies and minister obliged them to pay the town-officer eight pound Scots, is worthy of your Lordship and the rest of the Lords of the privy council's considerations; and it would be the height of charity to fall on a method to oblige the minister and baillies to refound it seven-fold.

Obs. 4th, One Thomas Brown, the only man accused by Patrick Morton, and imprisoned by the minister and baillies, after a great deal of hunger and hardship, died in prison, so as this poor woman's murder was not the first, neither will it be the last, unless by severe punishments prevented.

Obs. 5th, The baillies in a manner justified these two murthers, by not allowing them Christian burial, but burying them like dogs, scarce covering them from the ravens.

Obs. 6th, You may wonder why all along I should say the minister and baillies? The reason is, because during all this narrative he exercised more of the civil authority than any of the baillies, and so continues to do, as you may see by the following late instance.

The baillies of Pittenweem being conveened before the Lords of Privy Council on the 14th or 15th of February, I am informed gave in to them a subscribed account of the murther; and to justify themselves, assert they had imprisoned several of the murtherers before they left Pittenweem. It is very true they did so, but they were not long from the town when the minister set them at liberty. This, I think, is exercising the office of a civil magistrate: perhaps the minister may say he did it by the magistrates' order left behind them; then I think the magistrates were mightily in the wrong to give in to the Lords of the privy council an account they knew to be false.

My Lord, this is not the tenth part of what may be said upon this subject, I hope some other person will be more particular.

I am, My LORD, Your Lordship's Most humble servant.

An Account of an Horrd and Barbarous Murder, In a Letter from a Gentleman in Fife to his Friend in Edinburgh.

I doubt not of your being exceedingly surprized with this short and just account I give you of a most barbarous murder committed in Pittenweem the 30th of January last. One Peter Morton, a blacksmith in that town, after a long sickness, pretended that witches were tormenting him--that he did see them and know them--and, from time to time, as he declared such and such women to be witches, they were by order of the magistrates and minister of Pittenweem, apprehended as such, to a very considerable number, and put into prison. This man, by his odd postures and fits, which seemed to be very surprizing at first, wrought himself into such a credit with the people of that place, that unless the Earl of Rothes, our sheriff, had discovered his villany, and discouraged that practice, God knows how fatal it might have proved to many honest families of good credit and respect. Sir, however, at first many were deceived, yet now all men of sense are ashamed for giving any credit to such a person; but how hard it is to root out bad principles once espoused by the rabble, and how dangerous a thing it is to be at their mercy, will appear by the tragical account I give you of one of these poor women, Janet Corphat.

After she was committed prisoner to the tolbooth, upon a suspicion of her being a witch, she was well guarded with a number of men, who, by pinching her, and pricking her with pins, kept her from sleep many days and nights, threatening her with present death, unless she would confess herself guilty of witchcraft; which at last she did. This report spreading abroad, made people curious to converse with her upon the subject, who found themselves exceedingly disappointed. The Viscount of Primrose being in Fife occasionally, inclined to satisfy his curiosity in this matter, the Earl of Kellie, my Lord Lyon, the Laird of Scotstarvat, and the Laird of Randerston, were with his Lordship in Pittenweem. Three of the number went to the tolbooth and discoursed with her, to whom she said, that all that she had confessed, either of herself or her neighbours, were lies, and cried out, God forgive the minister, and said, that he had beat her one day with his staff when she was telling him the truth. They asked her how she came to say any thing that was not true; she cryed out, alas, alas, I behoved to say so, to please the minister and baillies; and, in the mean time, she begged for Christ's sake not to tell that she had said so, else she would be murdered. Another time, when the Laird of Glenagies and Mr Bruce of Kinross, were telling her, she needed not deny what they were asking her, for she had confessed as much as would infallibly burn her; she cried out, God forbid! and to one of the two she said, that from which he might rationally conclude, she insinuate she had assurance from the minister her life should not be taken.

A little before harvest, Mr Ker of Kippilaw, a writer to the signet, being in Pittenweem, Mr Robert Cook, advocate, went with him to prison to see this poor woman; Mr Cook, among other questions, asked her, if she had not renounced her baptism to the devil; she answered, she never renounced her baptism but to the minister. These were her words, what she meant by them I know not. The minister having got account of this from Mr Cook, he sent for her, and in presence of Mr Cook and Mr Ker in the church, he threatened her very severely, and commanded the keeper to put her into some prison by herself under the steeple, least (as he said) she should pervert those who had confessed. The keeper put her into a prison in which was a low window, out of which it was obvious that any body could make an escape; and, accordingly, she made her escape that night.

Next day when they missed her, they made a very slight search for her, and promised ten pound Scots to any body that would bring her back. Mr Gordon, minister at Leuchars, hearing she was in his parish, eight miles distant from Pittenweem, caused apprehend her, and sent her prisoner, under custody of two men, on the 30th of January, to Mr Cowper, minister of Pittenweem, without giving any notice to the magistrates of the place. When she came to Mr Cowper, she asked him if he had any thing to say to her? he answered, No. She could get lodging in no house but with one Nicolas Lawson, one of the women that had been called witches.--Some say a baillie put her there.

The rabble hearing she was in town, went to Mr Cowper, and asked him what they should do with her? he told them he was not concerned, they might do what they pleased with her. They took encouragement from this to fall upon the poor woman, those of the minister's family going along with them, as I hear; they fell upon the poor creature immediately, and beat her unmercifully, tying her so hard with a rope, that she was almost strangled; they dragged her through the streets, and alongst the shore, by the heels. A baillie, hearing of a rabble near his stair, came out upon them, which made them immediately disappear. But the magistrates, though met together, not taking care to put her into close custody for her safety, the rabble gathered again immediately, and stretched a rope betwixt a ship and the shore, to a great height, to which they tied her fast; after which they swinged her to and fro, from one side to another, in the mean time throwing stones at her from all corners, until they were weary; then they loosed her, and with a mighty swing threw her upon the hard sands, all about being ready in the mean time to receive her with stones and staves, with which they beat her most cruelly. Her daughter, in the time of her mother's agony, though she knew of it, durst not adventure to appear, lest the rabble had used her after the same manner, being in a house, in great concern and terror, out of natural affection for her mother, (about which the author was misinformed in the first edition.) They laid a heavy door upon her, with which they prest her so sore, that she cried out, to let her up for Christ's sake, and she would tell the truth. But when they did let her up, what she said could not satisfy them, and therefore, they again laid on the door, and with a heavy weight of stones on it, prest her to death; and to be sure it was so, they called a man with a horse and a sledge, and made him drive over her corpse backward and forward several times. When they were sure she was killed outright, they dragged her miserable carcase to Nicolas Lawson's house, where they first found her.

There was a motion made to treat Nicolas Lawson after the same manner immediately; but some of them being wearied with three hours sport, as they called it, said it would be better to delay her for another day's divertisement; and so they all went off.

It is said that Mr Cowper, in a letter to Mr Gordon, gave some rise to all this; and Mr Cowper, to vindicate himself, wrote to Mr Gordon, whose return says, if he were not going to Edinburgh, he would give him a double of his letter. It's strange he sent him not the principal. In the postscript, he assures him, he shall conceal it to meeting.

'Tis certain, that Mr Cowper, preaching the Lord's day immediately after, in Pittenweem, took no notice of the murder, which at least makes him guilty of sinful silence. Neither did Mr Gordon, in his letter to Mr Cowper, make any regret for it; and this some construe to be a justifying of the horrid wickedness in both.

We are perswaded the government will examine this affair to the bottom, and lay little stress upon what the magistrates or minister of Pittenweem will say to smooth over the matter, seeing it's very well known, that either of them could have quashed the rabble, and prevented that murder, if they had appeared zealous against it.

I am sorry I have no better news to tell you, God deliver us from those principles that tend to such practices.

I am, SIR, Your humble servant.

A Just Reproof to the False Reports and Unjust Calumnies, in the Foregoing Letters.

About the month of March last year, one Beatrix Laing, a woman of very bad fame, who had formerly been under process for using charms, and refusing to be reconciled to her neighbours, was debarred from the Lord's table, came to one Patrick Morton, a blacksmith, desiring him to make some nails, which he refused to do, because otherwise employed at that time. Upon which she went off muttering some threatening expressions. A little after, the said Patrick Morton, with another person in company, carrying some fish by the said Beatrix Laing's door, they saw a vessel with water placed at the door, with a burning coal in it. Upon which he was presently strucken with an impression that it was a charm designed against him, and upon this a little after he sickened. In this sickness he languished for a long time; physicians that saw him, could not understand his distemper, yet tried various medicines, till at length his trouble increased, and he began to be seized with some unusual fits, which made them give over. He forbore all this while any accusation of the person whom he all along suspected for his trouble, at least he made no mention of it to the minister, who frequently visited him while under it. But his trouble still increasing, he at length began to drop some apprehensions of the cause of it. Upon which Beatrix Laing was called, and by the magistrates, in the said Patrick Morton's father's house, examined in presence of a great multitude of people, and owned, that she had placed that vessel with water, and the coal in it, there; but at that time would give no account of the reason of it. Being dismissed by the magistrates, she went home, and that same night, when she was challenged by Katharine Marshal, in her own house, before Nicolas Lawson, about the lad's trouble, she answered, that he might blame his own ill tongue for what had befallen him, and that it was an evil spirit that was troubling him; which was in her face maintained by the said persons next day, in presence of the magistrates. Then the boy began to complain of her tormenting him, and fell into grievous fits of trouble upon her entering the house. Upon all which she being imprisoned, after some time did acknowledge to magistrates and minister, in presence of many witnesses, without threat or torture, (of which we shall speak more afterwards) that she was displeased with Patrick Morton for his refusing to make some nails; that she designed to be avenged upon him for it; and that she used that charm of the coal in the water against him; and that she renounced her baptism, entered into a compact with the devil some twelve years before; condescending upon time, place, and her inducements to engage in his service; and that she, with Nicholas Lawson, had made a wax picture to torment him, and put pins in it; which the said Nicolas likewise confessed afterwards, and so justified the boy's account of the rise of his trouble.

After this the boy's trouble daily increased, in which there were many strange things; first his belly, for some time, then his breast, frequently heaved up to a prodigious height, and instantly went off again, by a blowing at the mouth like a bellows; frequently he cried out that such persons as he named were pinching him in his arms, breast, or some other places of his body, his hands lying all the while above the clothes, at a distance from one another, in the view of many of the spectators; and when they looked the places of which he complained, they saw distinctly the print of nails. Again, he was frequently cast into swooning fits, became insensible, which was tried by exquisite pinching the more sensible parts of his body, of which he complained afterwards when he came out of the fits, though he took no notice of them, nor felt them, in the time while he was in these fits. The strongest who essayed to lift his head from the pillow, were not able to move it, though both his feet and head were perfectly free of the bed, which was exactly tried: Yea, sometimes while the trunk of his body and his head were thus rigid and could not be raised from the pillow, his legs were loose, and any might move them as they pleased. Sometimes these fits were not so great as at other times, and then, or when he was falling in, or coming out of them, several persons lifted him with little difficulty; but when he was in the depth of the fit, the strongest that essayed it could not raise him up. Again, when any of the women whom he accused touched him, and sometimes on their coming into the room he fell into grievous fits of trouble, and cried out, that such a person was tormenting him, condescending on their names; and this he did very frequently, before multitudes of people of different ranks, ready to attest the same. And commonly such care was taken to prevent his having any notice, either of the womens' entry, or which of them was there, that there was no place left for any rational suspicion of trick or cheat in the matter. He was carefully hoodwinked with several plies of cloth--the women were brought in with the utmost secrecy--innocent persons present in the room laid their hands on him, but yet he never shewed the least concern, save when the accused persons touched him. Several times gentlemen that seemed jealous that there was somewhat of an imposture in the case, were allowed and invited to make the nicest trial, and found it hold. Several pitiful cavils have been used about this, and other instances of the boy's trouble, which proceed either from ignorance of the circumstances of matter of fact, or gross inadvertency in not observing the several variations of the boy's case; which, had they been considered, they would have been so far from giving any countenance to the conclusion aimed at by these objectors, that they would strongly have enforced a conviction of something preter-natural in the case.

The author then proceeds to give an account of Janet Corphat, the woman who was murdered. She was a person of very bad fame, who of a long time was reputed a witch, frequently used charms, and was wont commonly to threaten persons who disobliged her, and such consequences sometimes followed, as made her the terror of many, both of the town and country, which might be verified by particular instances, if it were necessary. She was not at first delated by Patrick Morton, though afterwards he complained of her as one of his tormentors; but she, with several others, being in company with the devil, whereof Isabel Adam was one, in pursuance of a quarrel which Beatrix Laing, formerly mentioned, had with one Alexander M'Grigor, a fisher in the town, made an attempt to murder the said M'Grigor in bed; which was prevented by his awakening and wrestling against them. This attempt was acknowledged by Isabel Adam, of whose confession a more full account shall be given afterwards, who had been taken up on that man's delation, and some other informations against her, and not on the lad's. As likewise, the said Janet was accused by Nicolas Lawson, another person present at that attempt; and Nicolas accused her of being at another meeting in the Loan of Pittenweem; at both which meetings they confessed the devil was present.--All which she herself afterwards freely confessed.

The manner of this woman's confession was very remarkable.--After she had obstinately some while denied, and with a subtilty beyond what might be expected from one of her education, shifted all questions put to her, she, with Isobel Adam aforesaid, being brought to the house where the tormented lad lay, and he discovering her at her entry into the room, notwithstanding the utmost precaution was used to conceal it from him, and he falling into grievous fits of trouble, did cry out of her as one of his tormentors; at which she was so stunned, that instantly she fell a trembling. The magistrates and minister observing her in such a confusion, asked if she was willing to commune with them, in reference to the matters whereof she had been accused; she declaring herself willing, went with them to another place, and when desired to be ingenuous, she again fell a trembling, and said she would confess all, but was afraid the devil would tear the soul out of her body if she did, and said, if you will pray, and cause all good folk pray for me, I will confess, and she then desired the minister to pray; and, after prayer, confessed she was bodily present at both the meetings aforesaid with the devil and the witches, and gave a circumstantiat account of the renounciation of her baptism, naming time, place, and inducements which led her to it, and the shape the devil appeared to her in.--She likewise told the reason of their attempt to murder M'Grigor was, that he did not hire a house which belonged to Beatrix Laing.

Again, on a Thursday, after she had been hearing sermon, she desired to speak with the minister, and sent one to acquaint him with this desire; on which he went to her, and she, before several witnesses, renewed her former confession, and condescended on all the persons the other confessing witches had accused, as being present at the two foresaid meetings; adding withal, that there were others present whom she knew not. This confession she renewed before the presbytery, in presence of a great many country gentleman, and other spectators; as likewise in the face of a numerous congregation on the Lord's day.

It is owned, that when Beatrix Laing and Nicolas Lawson were first imprisoned, they were ill used by some of the guard, without the knowledge of magistrates or minister, of which the women made complaint to the minister, whereof he presently acquainted the magistrates, who, with the minister, went to the prison, and threatened the guard if they offered the least disturbance to persons in custody. And the minister, on the Lord's day thereafter, took occasion in sermon to discover the wickedness of that practice, as being against the light of nature, Scripture, and the just laws of the land. After this, we heard of no more disturbances they met with. Now, it was not till after this precaution used to prevent their trouble, that Janet Corphat was imprisoned; and, from the time of her imprisonment, till the time that she confessed, which was some ten or twelve days, she was not in company with the rest, nor with the guard, save one or two days, but was alone in a separate prison, and nothing to disturb her.

Now, it is remarkable, that neither of these persons who were ill used, of which Janet Corphat was none, did ever make any acknowledgement to these persons who used them ill, nor till some days after they were quite freed of this trouble. And when they did confess, it was to magistrates and minister, whom they owned to be careful to preserve them from such abuses; nor did magistrates or minister ever use any threatening to extort a confession, or any other argument, but what the gospel requires to be made use of to bring impenitent sinners to a confession of their sins.[8]

The author of the letter tells us, 'she was put in a low prison, out of which it was obvious that any body could make an escape, and accordingly she made her escape that night.' Here are but two assertions, and both of them false, for the prison was the second story, and her escape was by breaking an old iron grate in the window; nor was it that night after that she broke the prison, for it was on Friday these gentlemen discoursed her, and on the Lord's day at night she broke the prison.[9]

Here follows the author of the 'Just Reproofs' way of telling the story of the barbarous and cruel murder of Janet Corphat. She came to town under cloud of night with two men, and went straight to an inn where her daughter was serving. After some stay there, the two men brought her to the minister's house, who was visiting a sick child of one James Cook, a present bailie, where his servant came to him with Mr Gordon's letter; and, as soon as he had perused it, he bid his servant go tell them, he would have nothing to do with her, but since they had brought her to the town, let them take her to the magistrates; which answer, two men then present, have attested under their hands. On this, the men brought her to Bailie Cook's house, where the minister was, and the men meeting him coming down stairs, pressed him to take her off their hands, which he refused to do, but called the two next magistrates, and advised them instantly to set her off safe out of the town. On which the two bailies sent for their officer immediately, and the minister went off straight to his own house, and saw no appearance of a rabble, nor did hear of it, till the rabble had gone a considerable length; and after a little, he heard that the woman was got safe out of their hands, and the rabble dissipate, and he knew nothing of her death till the next morning.

When the officer came to the magistrates, they, on deliberation among themselves, resolved to imprison her till the next morning; and accordingly ordered their officer to do it. And as the officer was executing the magistrates' orders, the rabble gathered upon them, attacked the officer, and took the woman from him, with which, it is said, he did not acquaint the magistrates, that they might have taken other measures for the woman's safety.

This rabble did not flow from the inclinations of the people of the place, which is evident from the peaceable and safe residence two confessing witches had for two months time in the place since they were set at liberty, but from an unhappy occasional concourse of a great many strangers, some Englishmen, some from Orkney, and other parts, who were forward in it, and have since taken guilt on them by their flight.

As to the assertion with regard to those of Mr Cowper's family going along with the rabble, Mr Cowper urged to have his servants examined among the first, and they have declared before the magistrates, that they stole out in a clandestine way, that their master might not know of it, and he indeed knew nothing of it, and they returned very quickly and made no stay; nor do any of the witnesses examined insinuate any accusation of their having the least accession to any injury she met with, nor were they any other way concerned, than by looking on a short while with some hundreds of other spectators.

Again, it is said, 'that they first found her at Nicolas Lawson's house, and that she was killed outright when they dragged her there again,' is as ill grounded as the rest of our author's assertions; for they found her not at Nicolas Lawson's house, and some of the persons examined have declared, that after she was brought to that door, she arose and put on head cloaths, and called to Nicolas Lawson to let her in; which, if she had done, she in all appearance had met with no more disturbance; but after this, we hear that some few of the rabble stole up secretly and murdered her.

The author of the Second Letter accuses the minister of encouraging Patrick Morton in carrying on the cheat, by reading to him the case of Bargarran's daughter. In answer to which, we shall give a short, but candid, account of matter of fact. In the month of May last, the minister, with a preacher, and a great many other people, attending all night in the room where Patrick Morton lay, and he lying meanwhile in a swooning fit, which was then tried by exquisite pinching, the minister and probationer falling into some discourse about Bargarran's daughter, took out the book, and for their own satisfaction, read only two sentences, and stopt. Several weeks after, when the minister was again attending in the night time, the lad being insensible, the minister, for his own diversion, read the preface, and some part of the process, against the witches, but had no reason to think he heard any thing, but on the contrary. And it is to be observed, when the committee of the privy council did accurately examine the boy in reference to this story, he still declared he never heard any thing of Bargarran's daughter's case read.

What he says of 'their obliging them to pay eight pound Scots to the town-officer,' is in many ways false. It is false that they were ordered by the magistrates to pay such a sum. It is false that they paid all alike. It is also untruth that any of them gave what they had provided for their winding sheets. Nicolas Lawson, one of the confessing witches, her husband voluntarily gave a small piece of unbleached linen to the officer for his fees; and this is all the ground for the story of their winding-sheets.

The author of the Just Reproof then proceeds to give an account of Mrs White and Isobel Adam. The woman brought from Anstruther was a Mrs White, an inhabitant of Pittenweem, who, through fear of being apprehended, fled thither to her daughter's house. This woman, whose cause is now warmly espoused by some, with no advantage to their reputation, and who is now insisting against the magistrates in a process for wrongous imprisonment, has been for many years a person of very bad fame. Some eighteen years ago, she pursued a woman before the session, in Mr Bruce the late Episcopal incumbents time, for calling her a witch, and succumbing in the probation. Mr Bruce urged her to be reconciled with the woman,--she obstinately refused,--using most Unchristian and revengeful expressions, which are to be seen in the session-register. Since the revolution, she desired admission to the Sacrament of the Lord's Supper, which was then denied her, because she still refused to be reconciled to that woman. Her scandalous carriage in refusing to cohabit with her husband to this day, who is a sober honest man, is generally known. This woman being accused by the boy as one of his tormentors, and delated by two confessing witches, and other presumptions of her guilt, the magistrates one morning sent their officer to the magistrates of Anstruther, desiring them on these grounds to send Mrs White to them, and the grounds of her imprisonment were sent in write to her, in her daughter Mrs Lindsay's house; and she being brought to Pittenweem, the two women which delated her, were confronted with her, in presence of the magistrates, a great many gentlemen and ministers, where they did accuse her to her face, and charged her particularly with being at a meeting in the Loan with the devil and the witches, and gave some binding tokens to convince her. By all which it appears, how little ground there is to accuse the magistrates for invading their neighbours jurisdiction, or load the minister with any concernment in the matter.

As to the other instance of one brought to Pittenweem at six miles distance, this was the young woman Isobel Adam. About the middle of May, one Alexander M'Grigor delated her for an attempt to murder him in his own house in the night-time, with several others whom he knew not; and there being some surmises of other presumptions of witchcraft against her, the minister hearing she was occasionally in the town, called for her, and advised her, before her father, if innocent, to take proper measures for her own vindication, which she undertook to do, and promised to return for that end on advertisement, which her father engaged to give. The noise about her still increasing, her father was desired, according to promise, to call her to the place, which he declined, growing jealous of her guilt; on which the minister advertised her, but in case she refused, a letter was sent to be delivered to the gentleman on whose ground she lived, desiring him to send her. So soon as the advertisement was given, she came voluntarily to her father's house in Pittenweem, and so there was no occasion for force.

When she came, she confessed her converse with the devil at Thomas Adamson's house, on the first day of January 1704; she was confronted with M'Grigor, and he accused her of the above mentioned attempt on him, which she then refused; on which she was imprisoned, and the two following days, she did with tears, and more than ordinary concern, make a free and large confession.

She said Beatrix Laing aforesaid, a confessing witch, had been dealing with her to engage in her service, which she refused; and that some time thereafter, this Beatrix came for her, and desired her to go along to her house; when she came there, they sat down at the fire, and she saw a man in black cloaths, with a hat on his head, sitting at the table; and Beatrix said to her, since you will not engage with me, here is a gentleman that will see you; whereupon he told her, he knew she was discontented with her lot, and if she would serve him, he promised she should want for nothing; to which she yielded to serve him, and he came forward and kissed her; and she said, he was fearsome like, and his eyes sparkled like candles, on which she knew he was the devil.

Again, she told, that being employed to spin in Thomas Adamson's house in Pittenweem, while she was lying awake in her bed in the night time, the devil appearing to her, where she did expressly renounce her baptism to the devil, by putting her hand on her head, and the other to her feet, the other maid lying in the bed with her being at the time asleep, as the maid declared before the session. About a fortnight after this, Beatrix Laing came to visit her, and asked her, if she had met with the gentleman? She answered she had, and also engaged with him, on which Beatrix said, I have then got my work wrought, and went away. And she confessed, she came to that meeting at M'Grigor's with the devil and several witches, viz. Beatrix Laing, Nicolas Lawson, Janet Corphat, Thomas Brown, and several others she knew not, designing to murder M'Grigor; but since the man awakened and prayed to God for himself, they could not do it. She confessed also converse with the devil at other times. All which is in her two confessions, signed by the magistrates, and transmitted to Edinburgh. Now, we desire to know what the author of this letter can quarrel in the magistrates or minister's conduct in this matter.

As for what he says 'about the magistrates and minister refounded the imprisoned womens' money seven-fold.' We find this author very charitable on other mens' purses, but when the magistrates and minister design to bestow their charity, they will choose more deserving objects. And the Lords of Her Majesty's privy counsel understands themselves better than to take their measures as to what is just from the daring prescriptions of this author.

What he says about Thomas Brown is also false, he was accused by the lad, and delated by three confessing witches, as being accessory to the attempt on M'Grigor. It is false he was starved, for his daughter brought him his diets punctually. Our author's fears of more murders are altogether groundless, and we appeal to all men of candour, whether this author's impudent and unjust accusation against magistrates and minister of murdering Thomas Brown, deserves not severer punishment than any thing he can charge them with.

He again tells us, "the bailies justified the murder, by denying Christian burial." The bailies gave no order thereabout. As for Thomas Brown, his son-in-law, with some others, buried him. Our author by his next may prove, that Janet Corphat, a woman that had so frequently and so solemnly confessed the renounciation of her baptism to the devil, deserved Christian burial.

THE END.

Footnotes:

8. We should like to know what threatenings the gospel requires ministers to make use of to such impenitent sinners as will not confess sins they could not commit. ED.

9. This just reprover begins very fairly by wilfully perverting his opponent's language, 'a prison with a low window,' he makes 'a low prison.' We very much suspect the minister himself had a hand in this pamphlet.

A COPY OF THE INDICTMENT OF THE WITCHES AT BORROWSTOUNESS--THE PRECEPT FOR SUMMONING THE JURY AND WITNESSES--WITH THE WARRANT FOR THEIR EXECUTION.

Copy of the Indytment.

Annaple Thomsone, widow in Borrowstownes,
Margaret Pringle, relict of the deceast John Campbell sive-wright there, &c.

Yee, and ilk ane of yow ar indytted and accwsed, that where, notwithstanding, be the law of God, particularlie sett down in the 20 chapter of Leviticus, and eighteen chap. of Dewtronomie, and be the lawes and actes of parliament of this kingdome, and constant practiq; thereof, particularlie be the 73 act, 29 parliament Q. Marie, the cryme of witchcraft is declaired to be ane horreid, abominable and capitall cryme, punishable with the paines of death and confiscatiown of moveables. Never the less it is of veritie, that you have comitted, and ar gwyltie of the said cryme of witchcraft, in swa far ye have entered in pactiown with the devill, the enemie of your salvatiown, and have renownced our Blissed Lord and Savior, and your baptizme, and have given your selffes, both soulles and bodies to the devil, and have bein severall mettings with the devill, and swndrie wyth witches in diverse places; and particularlie, ye the said Annaple Thomsone had a metting with the devill the tyme of your weidowhood, befoer yow was maried to your last husband, in your cwming betwixt Linlithgow and Borrowstownes, where the devil, in the lyknes of ane black man, told yow, that you wis ane poore puddled bodie, and had ane evill lyiff, and difficultie to win throw the world; and promesed, iff yee wald followe him, and go alongst with him, yow should never want, bot have ane better lyiff: and, abowt fyve wekes therefter, the devill appeired to yow when yow wis going to the coal-hill abowt sevin a clock in the morning. Having renewed his former tentatiown, you did condeschend thereto, and declared yowrselff content to follow him, and becwm his servant; wherewpon the devill threw yow to the grownd, and had carnal copwlatiown with yow; and ye, and each persone of yow, wis at several mettings with the devill in the Linkes of Borrowstowness, and in the howss of yow Bessie Vickar, and ye did eatt and drink with the devill, and with on another, and with witches in hir howss in the night tyme; and the devill and the said Wm Craw browght the ale which ye drank, extending to abowt sevin gallons, from the howss of Elizabeth Hamilton; and yow the said Annaple had ane other metting abowt fyve wekes ago, when you wis going to the coal-hill of Grange, and he inveitted yow to go alongest and drink with him in the Grange-pannes; and yow the said Margaret Pringil have bein ane witch thir many yeeres bygane; hath renowncid yowr baptisme, and becwm the devill's servant, and promeis to follow him; and the devill had carnall copwlatiown with yow, and tuik you by the right hand, whereby it was, for eight dayes, grevowslie pained; but having it twitched of new againe, it imediatlie becam haill: and yow the said Margaret Hamilton has bein the devill's servant these eight or nyne yeres bygane; and he appered and conversed with yow at the toun-well of Borrowstownes, and several tymes in yowr awin howss, and drank severall choppens of ale with you, and thereafter had carnall copwlatiown with yow; and the devill gave yow ane fyve merk peice of gold, whilk a lyttil efter becam ane sklaitt stone; and yow the said Margaret Hamilton, relict of James Pollwart, has bein ane witch, and the devil's servant thertie yeres since, haith renowncid yowr baptizme as said is, and has had carnall copwlatiown with the devill in the lyknes of ane man, bot he removed from yow in the lyknes of ane black dowg: and ye, and ilk ane of yow wis at ane metting with the devill and wther witches at the Croce of Murestaine above Kinneil, upon the thretttein of October last, where yow all danced, and the devill acted the pyiper, and where yow endevored to have distroyed Androw Mitchell, sone to John Mitchell, elder in Dean of Kinneill.

Precept qra Witches, and the Witnesses and Assyissers, 1679.
---- Cochran of Barbbachlay, Richard Elphinstown of ----, Saindelands of Hilderstown, ---- Cornwal of Bonhard, Robert Hamilton of Dechmont, baillzie of the regallitie of Borrowstownes, Sir John Harper advocat, Mr William Dundas, and Mr John Prestowne advocats, commissioners of

justiciarie, speciallie constitwte, nominat, and appoynted by the lordes off his majestie's most honowrable privie cownsell for the tryall and jwdging of the persones after namit; To our lovitts ---- messengers, macers, and officers of cowrt, owr shirriffs in that pairt, conjunctlie and severallie, speciallie constitwte, greitting: For sameikillais the ---- day of ----is appoynted by ws for the trying and judging off Anabill Thomson widow in Borrowstownes, Margaret Pringle relict of the decist John Campbell sive-wright ther, Margaret Hamilton relict of the deceist James Pollwart ther, Wm. Craw indweller ther, Bessie Viccar relict of the deceist James Pennie indweller ther, and Margarett Hamilton relict of the deceist Thomas Mitchell, who are apprehendit and imprisoned in the tolbuith of Borrowstownes, as suspect gwilty of the abominable cryme of witchcraft, by entering into pactioun with the devill, renwncing their baptism and comitting of malificies: Wherefoir nescessary it is, that the saides persones should be summonded to wnderlye the lawe for the samen, and that witness and assyssers should be cited against them, to the effect, and under the paines efter specifiet. HEREFOIR, this precept sein, we chairge you passe, and in owr soveraigne lordes name and authority, and owrs, comand and chairge the saides persones above compleaned upon, to compeir befoir ws, or any three of us (who are by our said commissiown declaired to be a quorum), within the said tolbuith of Borrowstownes, the nyneteen day of December nixt, in the howr of cawse, ther to wnderlye the lawe, for the crymes above specifiet, and that under the paines contained in the new acts of parliament: And sicklyik, summon, wairne and chairge ane assyse of honest and famous persones, not exceeding the number of fortie-five, togither with such witnesses who best know the veritie of the persones above compleaned upon ther gwiltynes, to compeir befoir us, day and place foirsaid, in the howr of cawse, the persones of[10] witness, to bear leall and soothfast witnessing in the premiss, and the inqueist to passe upon the assyse each persone, under the paine of ane hundreth merks, according to justice, ais ye will answer to us therwpon: the whilk to doe commits to you, conjunctlie and severalie, our fwll power, be thir our lettres, delyvering them be you dewllie execut and indorset againe to the beirer. Given under our hands at Borrowstownes, the twentie-nynt day of November, ane thousande six hunder and seventie nyne yeirs.

(Sic Subscribitur)

R. HAMILTON,
J. CORNWALL,
RICH. ELPHENSTONE,
W. DUNDAS.

    Ane List of the Persones to be warned to passe upon the Assyse for Judging the Witches in Borrowstownes.

Barronie of Carridin.

    Robert Ballendin elder in Northbank,
    Alex. Brown in Bonhard,
    John Irwyne there,
    James Lamb there,
    George Storie in Mure-edge,
    Thomas Knox wiver in Littill Carridin,
    John Meldrum ther,
    George Yowng in Murrayes,
    John Brown oversman ther,
    George Smyth ther,
    John Robertsone in Bonhard-panns,
    John Daviesone ther,
    John Pooll ther.

Town of Borrowstownes.

    George Bennet,
    James Cassilles elder, skipper,
    Alex. Drysdaill skipper,
    James Hardie glover,
    Alex. Randie baxter
    Richard Carss,
    James Hamilton elder,
    James Hwtton baxter,

Andrew Hamilton,
Thomas Downie,
James Mwngill wiver,
Rob. Downie.

Barronie of Kinneill.

George Gib in Kinneil Carss,
Alex. Gib in Inneraven,
John Glen ther
John Baird ther
James Dobbie in Nether Kinneil,
Patrick Hardie ther,
John Dick in Woodheid,
John Wilson in Over Kinneil,
James Thomson ther,
James Lithgow in Balderstown,
John Hardie, maltman in Burrowstown,
James Thomson ther.

Barronie of Pollmont.

James Burn of Clerkstoun,
James Monteth of Myln-hall,
Alex. Whyte in Hill,
Patrick Ballanden of Parkend,
John Mairschell in Whyteside,
Andrew Johnstown in Pollmont,
David Ballanden in Redding,
James Gaff ther,
George Mureheid ther,
William Rwchat of Ruch-haugh,
John Grintown in Gillstown Loanfoote,
Henry Taylor in Whyteside,
John Purgat of Bruchtown Crag.

Order and Warrand for Burning the Witches of Borrowstownes, Dec. 19, 1679.

Forsameikle as Annabil Thomson widdow in Borrowstownes, Margaret Pringle relict of the deceast John Campbell ther, Margaret Hamiltown relict of the deceast James Pollwart ther, William Craw indweller ther, Bessie Wicker relict of the deceast James Pennie ther, and Margaret Hamiltown relict of the deceast Thomas Mitchell ther, prisoners in the tolbuith of Borrowstownes, are found guiltie be ane assyse, of the abominable cryme of witchcraft committed be them, in maner mentioned in their dittayes, and are decerned and adjudged be us under subscryvers (commissioners of justiciary speciallie appoynted to this effect) to be taken to the west end of Borrowstownes, the ordinar place of execution ther, upon Tuesday the twentie-third day of December current, betwixt two and four a clock in the efternoon, and ther to be wirried at a steack till they be dead, and there-efter to have their bodies burnt to ashes. These therefoir require and command the baylie principal off the regalitie of Borrowstownes, and his deputts, to see the said sentance and doom put to dew execution in all poynts, as yee will be answerable. Given under our hands at Borrowstownes the nynteenth day of December 1679 yeirs.

W. DUNDAS,
RICH. ELPHINSTONE,
WA. SANDILANDS,
J. CORNWALL,
J. HAMILTON.

Footnotes:

10. This word is interlined, and the word inqueist scored out.

TRIAL OF ISOBEL ELLIOT, AND NINE OTHER WOMEN.

Records of Justiciary, September 13, 1678.

In 1678, Isobel Elliot and nine other women were tried for witchcraft in one day. The articles of indictment against all of them were pretty much the same. Those exhibited against Isobel Elliot were as follows: That about two years ago she staid at home from the kirk at the desire of her mistress, who was a witch, when the devil had a meeting with the prisoner, her mistress, and two other witches; that he kissed the prisoner, baptized her on the face with an waff of his hand like a dewing, and offered to lie with her, but forbore because she was with child; that after she was kirked the devil often met her, and had carnal copulation with her. The prisoner and the other nine miserable women underwent all the legal forms incident to their unhappy situation among that deluded and barbarous people. They had been prosecuted by his Majesty's Advocate; they judicially acknowledged their guilt, were convicted by the jury, condemned by the judges, and burned by the executioner,--for having had carnal copulation with the devil!!!

THE CONFESSIONS OF HELEN TAYLOR IN EYEMOUTH, AND MENIE HALYBURTON IN DIRLTON, ACCUSED OF WITCHCRAFT, 1649.

WITH THE DECLARATION OF JOHN KINCAID, PRICKER. COPIED FROM THE ORIGINALS. THE CONFESSIOUN OF HELENE TAILZEAR.

JUL 8, 1649.

    Being the Sabbath day, Mr Samuel Dowglas, preaching at Eymouth, after sermon, Helen Tailzear desyred to speik with the said Mr Samuell, who coming to hir, thair being also present Samuel Lauder and George Halliday, she confessed these particularis, viz. first, at Candilmas bygon two yeirs, scho cam into Isobell Brown's hous, quhair the divill was sitting in the liknes of a gentill man at the tabill drinking with Isobell Brown, who took hir in his armes without any moir speiking at that tyme.

    Secondlie, Scho declairs, that after shee cam to Isobell Brown's hous * * * * * whair the divill was in the same likness as befor, and layd his hand upon hir head, and sayd, you sall be on of myne so long as you live. And that he gave hir two dolleris, and when shoe cam home they wer butt twa stanes.

    Thirdlie, Shee declairs, that shee was at ane meiting with Isobell Brown, Alison Cairns, Margaret Dobson, and Beatrix Young, and that thai went all along to William Burnettis hous, he lying sick, and that coming to the hous, Margaret Dobson was in the liknes of ane black hen, and went in at the chimley head, and Beatrix Young in the liknes of a litill foall, and that hirself was in the liknes of ane litill quhelp; Isobell Brown wes in hir owin liknes, with a long tail'd courtshaw upon hir head, and Allison Cairns wes in hir owin liknes; and that Isobell Brown desired her to go into William Burnettis bot shee refuissed, quhairupon Isobell Brown did stryk her * * * * * on the back.

    Fourtlie, Shee declairs that Marioun Robisson wes ane witch, and that shee was William Burnit's death.

(Signed) MR SAMUEL DOUGLAS, Minister at Coldinghame.
S. LAUDER.
G. HALLIDAY.

THE DEPOSITION OF MENIE HALIBURTOUN.

At Dirltoun, June, 1649.

    Compeirit Menie Halliburton, prissoner within the Castle, suspect of the cryme of witchcraft, delaitit guiltie be Agnes Clerkson, lait sufferer for the said cryme; as also be Patrik Watsone, spouse to the said Menie, who lykewisse sufferit thairfoir, and confessit, that auchtein yeir syne, or thairby, hir dochter being seik, scho first sent for Patrik Chrystison in Aberledie, to cum and cure hir dochter, and he refuising, went hirself for him, who refused to cure hir; and within * * * days after came the devill in liknes of a man into hir hous, calling himself a physition, and said to her, that he had good salves (and namelie oylispek), whairwith he would cure hir dochter; and aggreing with him for some of his salves quhilk he gave hir, shee gave him two Inglis shillings. He then departed, and promised to come agane within eight dayis, whilk accordinglie he did, bot or he went away the first tyme, shee gave him milk and breid; and Patrik Watsone coming in, he sent for a pynt of ale; bot at his second coming he stayit all night, and upon the morne airlie (Patrick being furth), in cam the divill and lay doun with hir, scho being yitt in bed, and had carnal copulatioun with hir, his nature being cald. He desyrit hir to renunce Chryst and hir baptisme, and become his servant, quhilk scho did. And sayis, that hir dochter had the wyte of all hir wickit wissing, and wissing she had nevir beene borne.

    This deposition was renewed in all the particulars by the said Menie, in the foresaid place, on Sunday the first of July, 1649, before Alexander Levingston of Saltcoatts, James Borthwick chamberlane, James Lawder, John Stalker baillie, Wm. Dalzell, and Mr John M'Ghie, minister at Dirltoun.

(Signed) J. MAKGHIE.
ALEX. LEVINGSTOUN, witness.
JA. BORTHWICK.
JAMES LAUDER.
JOHN STALKER.
W. DALZELL.
WALTER MARSHALL.

THE DECLARATION OF JOHN KINCAID.

JUNE, 1649.

    The whilk day, in presence of Alex. Levingston of Saltcoattis, James Borthwick chalmerlain of Dirltoun, John Stalker baillie thairof, James Foirman in Drem, Mr James Achieson in North-Berwick, and William Dalzell notar, Patrick Watson in West Fenton, and Menie Haliburtoun his spous, bruitted and long suspect of witchcraft, of thair awin frie will uncompellit, heiring that I John Kincaid under subscryvand wes in the toune of Dirltoune, and had some skill and dexterity in trying of the divillis marke in the personis of such as wer suspect to be witches, came to the broad hall in the Castell of Dirltoune, and desyred me the said John Kincaid to use my tryall of thame as I had done on utheris, whilk when I had done, I found the divillis marke upon the bak syde of the said Patrik Watsone, a littill under the point of his left shoulder, and upon the left syde of the said Menie Halyburtoun hir neck a littill above her left shoulder, whairof thay wer not sensible, neither cam furth thairof any bloode after I had tryed the samin as exactlie as ever I did any uthers. This I testifie to be of veritie upon my credit and conscience. In witnes quhairof, I have subscryvit thir presentis with my hand, day and place forsaid, befoir ther witnesses above specifiet.

J. K.

ALEX. LEVINGSTOUN, witness.
JA. BORTHWICK, witness.
JOHN STALKER, witness.
JAMES FORMAN, witness.
JA. ACHESONE, witness.
W. DALZELL, witness.

THE TRIAL OF WILLIAM COKE AND ALISON DICK, FOR WITCHCRAFT.

Extracted from the Minutes of the Kirk-Session of Kirkaldy, A. D. 1636.

September 6th, 1633.

The which day, compeared Alison Dick, challenged upon some speeches uttered by her against William Coke, tending to witchcraft,--denied the samyne.

    1. Compeared Alexander Savage, Andrew Nicol, and George Tillie, who being admitted and sworn, deponed as follows: The said Alexander Savage, that he heard the said Alison Dick say to her husband William Coke, 'Thou has put down many ships; it had been gude for the people of Kirkaldie, that they had knit a stone about thy neck and drowned thee.'
    2. Andrew Nicol deponed, that he heard the said Alison say to him, 'Thou has gotten the woman's song laid, as thou promised; thou art over-long living; it had been gude for the women of irkaldy, that thou had been dead long since. I shall cause all the world wonder upon thee.'
    3. George Tillie deponed, that he heard her say to him, 'It had been gude for the women of Kirkaldy, to put him to death; and that he had died seven years since.'

Also compeared Jean Adamson, Kathrine Spens, Marion Meason, Isobel Murison, Alison Kelloch, who being admitted and sworn, deponed as follows:

    4. Jean Adamson deponed, that she heard Alison Dick say to her husband William Coke, 'Thief! Thief! what is this that I have been doing? keeping the thretty years from meikle evil doing. Many pretty men has thou putten down both in ships and boats; thou has gotten the woman's song laid now. Let honest men puddle and work as they like, if they please not thee well, they shall not have meikle to the fore when they die.'
    5. Kathrine Spens deponed, that she heard her say to him, 'Common thief, I have hindered thee from many ill turns doing, both to ships and boats.'
    6. Marion Meason deponed, that she heard her say, 'Common thief, mony ill turn have I hindered thee from doing thir thretty years; mony ships and boats has thou put down; and when I would have halden the string to have saved one man, thou wald not.'
    7. Isobel Murison deponed, that she heard her say to him, 'Thief, thief, I have keeped thee from doing many ill turnes. Thou has now laid the woman's song.'

September 24th, 1633.

    8. Compeared Janet Allan, relict of umquhile John Duncan fisher, deponed, that Alison Dick came in upon a certain time to her house, when she was lying in of a bairn, and craved some sour bakes; and she denying to give her any, the said Alison said, your bairns shall beg yet, (as they do.) And her husband being angry at her, reproved her; and she abused him in language; and when he strak her, she said, that she should cause him rue it; and she hoped to see the powarts bigg in his hair; and within half a year he was casten away, and his boat, and perished.
    9. Janet Sauders, daughter-in-law to the said William Coke and Alison Dick, deponed, that William Coke came in to her, and she being weeping, he demanded the cause of it, she answered, it was for her husband. The said William said, What ails thee? Thou wilt get thy gudman again, but ye will get him both naked and bare; and whereas there was no word of him for a long time before, he came home within two days thereafter, naked and bare as he said; the ship wherein he was being casten away.
    4, 10. Jean Adamson deponed, that when her gudman sailed with David Robertson, the said David having sent him home with a ship to come for Scotland, there was a long time that there was no word of that ship; so that David Robertson coming home, and the other ship not come, nor no word from her, he said he would never see her. The said Alison Dick came in to her, (she with her bairns being weeping), and said, What ails ye Jean to weep? She answered, We have all good cause to weep for my husband, whom we will never see more. The said Alison said, hold your tongue, your gudman and all the

company are well enough; they are in Norway loading their ship with timber to come home, they will be here shortly. And so it fell out in every point as she said.

5, 11. Kathrine Spens deponed, that William Coke came in to her, after that his wife had spoken so much evil to him, and said, Kathrine, my wife has spoken meikle ill of me this day, but I said nothing to her again. If I had spoken two words to her the last time she was in the steeple, she would never have gotten out of it.

***

Minutes of 24th September, ordains Mr James Miller to ride to Preston for the man that tries the witches. The expence to be paid by the Town and Session.

September 8th,

12. Compeared Isobel Hay, spouse to Alexander Law, against Alison Dick, who being sworn, deponed, that she having come in to her house, her husband being newly sailed, she craved some money of her, which she refused, and boasted her. The said Alison said, It shall gang wair geats; and that same voyage, her husband had great loss. And thereafter, the said Alison came in to her house, she being furth, and took her sister by the hand, and since that time, the maiden had never been in her right wits.

13. William Bervie declared, that Robert Whyt having once stricken William Coke, Alison Dick his wife, came to the said Robert, and said, Wherefore have ye stricken my husband? I shall cause you rue it. The said Robert replying, What sayest thou? I shall give you as much--you witch. She answered, 'Witches take the wit and the grace from you;' and that same night, he was bereft of his wits.

14. Janet Whyt, daughter to the said Robert, compearing, affirmed the said dittay to be true upon her oath. And added, that she went to the said Alison, and reproved her, laying the wyt of her father's sickness upon her. Let him pay me then, and he will be better; but if he pay me not, he will be worse; for there is none that does me wrong, but I go to my god and complains upon them, and within 24 hours I will get amends of them. The said Janet Whyt declared, that Alison Dick said to her servant, Agnes Fairlie, I have gotten a grip of your gudwife's thigh; I shall get a grip of her leg next; the said Janet having burnt her thigh before with lint: and thereafter she has taken such a pain in her leg, that she can get no remedy for it. Whilk the said Agnes Fairlie deponed upon her great oath to be true.

15. Alison Dick herself declared, that David Paterson, skipper, having struck William Coke her husband, and drawn him by the feet, and compelled him to bear his gear aboard, the said William cursed the said David, and that voyage he was taken by the Dunkirkers. Also, at another time thereafter, he compelled him to bear his gear aboard, and a captain's who was with him, and when the captain would have paid him, the said David would not suffer him; but he himself gave him what he liked. The said William cursed the said David very vehemently; and at that time he himself perished, his ship, and all his company, except two or three. Also she declared, that when his own son sailed in David Whyt's ship, and gave not his father his bonnallie,[11] the said William said, What? Is he sailed, and given me nothing? The devil be with him; if ever he come home again, he shall come home naked and bare; and so it fell out. For John Whyt, who had that ship freighted to Norway, and another wherein himself was, declared, that they had very foul weather; and the ship wherein the said young William Coke was, perished; and he saved all the men in the ship wherein he was himself. And albeit the storm increased two days before the perishing of the said ship, and six days after, yet the two hours space in which they were saving the men, it was so calm in that part of the sea, that they rowed from one ship to the other with two oars, and the sea was all troublesome about them. And the said William Coke the younger, was the first man that came a shipboard.

***

Paction.--The same day, Alison Dick being demanded by Mr James Simson, minister, when, and how, she fell in covenant with the devil? She answered, her husband mony times urged her, and she yielded only two or three years since. The manner was thus--He gave her, soul and body, quick and quidder full to the devil, and bade her do so. But she in her heart said, God guide me. And then she said to him, I shall do any thing that ye bid me: and so she gave herself to the devil in the foresaid words.-- This she confessed about four hours at even, freely, without compulsion, before Mr James Simson, minister, William Tennent, baillie, Robert French, town-clerk, Mr John Malcolme, schoolmaster, William Craig, and me, the said Mr James Miller, writer hereof.

October 15th.

16. The which day, compeared Christian Ronaldson, against Alison Dick, who, in her presence being sworn, deponed, that she having set an house to the said Alison, and when the gudman came

home he was angry, and said, he would not have the devil to dwell above him in the closs; and he went and struck up the door, and put forth the chimney that she put in it. And thereafter, Alison came to the said Christian, and chopped upon her shoulder, and said to her, Christie, your gudman is going to sail, and he has ane stock among his hands, but ere long, his stock shall be as short as mine. And so it fell out, for he was casten away in David Whyt's ship, and saved nothing.

October 22d.

17. Compeared Merjory Marshall, against Alison Dick, who being sworn, deponed, that Alison having brought her gudman's cloaths once from the Castle-haven,[12] she offered her 12d for her labour, who would not have it; and she said to her, Alison, there is not many of them. She answered, they shall be fewer the next time; and the next voyage he was cast away in David Whyt's ship.

18. Compeared also Kathrine Wilson, who being sworn, deponed, that she and Janet Whyt being sliding together, Alison Dick came to them, and asked silver from Janet Whyt, who would give her none, but fled her company into the said Kathrine's house, and she followed, and she gave her a piece bread, and Janet Whyt bade her give her a plack also, and she should pay her again. And when she got it, she said, Is this all that she gives me? If she had given me a groat, it would have vantaged her a thousand punds. This is your doing, evil tidings come upon you. And she went down the closs, and pissed at their meal-cellar door; and after that, they had never meal in that cellar, (they being meal makers.) And thereafter they bought a horse at 40 lib., and the horse never carried a load to them but two, but died in the batts, louping to death, so that every body said that he was witched.

October 29th.

19. Euphen Boswell being sworn, deponed, that her gudman being to sail to the East country, loaden with salt, the said Alison Dick having born some of the salt aboard, she came to her and craved money from her, who gave her meat, but would give her no money, saying to her, Alison, my gudman has paid you himself, and therefore, I will give you nothing. She replied, Will ye give me nothing? I hope in God it will be better sharp (cheaper) sold nor it was bought: and so it fell out, for the ship sailed upon the morn, and the day after that, she sank, salt and all, except the men, who were saved by another ship that was near by them.

20. Thomas Mustard being sworn, deponed, that James Wilson going once to sail, Alison Dick came to him, and desyred silver from him, he would give her none; she abused him with language, and he struck her; she said to him, that that hand should do him little good that voyage; and within two days after, his hand swelled as great as a pint-stoup, so that he could get little or nothing done with it. The next time also when he was to sail, the said Alison went betwixt him and the boat; and he said, Yon same witch thief is going betwixt me and the boat, I must have blood of her; and he went and struck her, and bled her, and she cursed him and banned him; and that same voyage, he being in Caithness, standing upon the shore cleithing a tow, and a boy with him, the sea came and took him away, and he died; and the boy was well enough.

***

Desires Mr Robert Douglas[13] to go to the Archbishop with this process, to get his approbation thereto, who takes upon him to do the same.

Minute of November 19th.--5s. given for a load of coals to Alison Dick;--14s. for her entertainment this week bygone, being this day, with her husband William Coke, burnt for witchcraft.

In the minute of 17th December, there is a particular account of the Town and Session's extraordinary Debursements for William Coke and Alison Dick, Witches.

In primis.--To Mr James Miller, when he went to Prestowne for a man to try them, 47s. £2 7
Item.--To the man of Culross, (the executioner) when he went away the first time, 12s. 0 12
Item.--For coals for the witches, 24s. 1 4
Item.--In purchasing the commission, 9 3
Item.--For one to go to Finmouth for the laird to sit upon their assise as judge, 0 6
Item.--For harden to be jumps to them, 3 10
Item.--For making of them, 0 8

Summa for the kirk's part £17 1 Scots.

The Town's part of Expenses Debursed extraordinarily upon William Coke and Alison Dick.

In primis.--For ten loads of coals to burn them, 5 merks, £3 6 8
Item.--For a tar barrel, 14s. 0 14 0
Item.--For towes, 0 6 0
Item.--To him that brought the executioner, 2 18 0
Item.--To the executioner for his pains, 8 14 0
Item.--For his expenses here, 0 16 4
Item.--For one to go to Finmouth for the laird, 0 6 0

Summa town's part, £17 1 0 Scots.
Both, 34 11 0

The following account is a voucher of a payment made by Alexander Louddon, a factor on the estate of Burncastle, the proprietor being then a minor and infant. It is entered in the factor's books thus:

***

Mair for Margarit Dunhome the time sche was in prison, and was put to death, 065: 14: 4.

***

Count gifin out be Alexander Louddon in Lylstoun, in ye yeir of God 1649 yeiris, for Margrit Dollmoune in Burncastell.

***

Item, in ye first, to Wm. Currie and Andrew Gray for the watching of hir ye space of 30 days, inde ilk day, xxx sh inde xlv lib Scotts
Item mair to Jon Kinked; for brodding of her[14] vi lib Scotts
Mair for meat and drink and wyne to him and his man iiij lib Scotts
Mair for cloth to hir iij lib Scotts
Mair for twa tare treis xl sh Scotts
Item mair for twa treis, and ye making of them to the workmen iij lib Scotts
Item to ye hangman in Hadingtoun, and fetchin of him, thrie dollores for his pens, is iiij lib xiiii sh
tem mair for meit and drink and wyne for his intertinge iii lib Scotts
Item mair fer ane man and twa horss, for ye fetcheing of him, and taking of him hame agane xl sh Scotts
Mair to hir for meit and drink ilk ane day, iiij sh the space of xxx dayes, is vi lib Scotts
Item mair to ye twa officers for yr fie ilk day sex shilline aught pennes, is x lib Scotts
Summa is iiij scoir xii lib xiiij sh

GHILBERT LAUDER.
UM. LAUDER BILZAURS.

Takin of this above written soume twentie-seaven pundis Scotis qlk the said umql Margrit Dinham had of her ain.

92: 14: --
27: --: --

65: 14: --

Footnotes:
11. His farewell cup.
12. Probably Ravenscraig Castle, at the east end of Pathhead. ED.
13. Who preached the famous coronation sermon of Charles II. at Scone, January 1st 1651.
14. See his declaration.

MINUTES AND PROCEEDINGS OF THE SESSION OF TORRYBURN, IN FIFESHIRE, CONCERNING WITCHCRAFT. WITH THE CONFESSION OF LILLIAS ADIE.

TAKEN FROM THE SESSION RECORDS MINUTES, &c.

Torry, June 30th, 1704.

    SEDERUNT, WM. HUTTON, WM. DALGLISH, WM. REID, JOHN MITCHELL, DAVID CURRY, GEO. TILLOCH, WITH THE MINISTER.

    The session being called, pro re nata, upon a flagrant rumour, that Jean Bizet, wife to James Tanochie, had been molested by Satan, and had complained of some particular person of the devil's instruments in that trouble that she lay under. Whereupon the minister ordered the officer to cite the said Jean Bizet, also Lilias Adie and Janet Whyte, whom she was said to complain of; and also to cite Mary Wilson, who is said to have taken the charm by stroking up her head; and also, he ordered the officer to cite Tanochie's daughter, with James Tanochie, James Whyte and his wife, Helen Anderson, and Mary Nielson, who are said to know something of the circumstances of that affair.

    1mo, Jean Bizet being called, compeared not, upon which the officer is ordered to cite her to the next.

    2do, There being a public report that Janet Whyte should have threatened James Tanochie's family with a mischief, but particularly his wife, before this befell; the said Janet was called, and interrogate, if ever she threatened James Tanochie's wife, she declares, that she never threatened any such thing, nor thought so. Moreover, she said, that James his wife would not say so, otherwise she would lay down her head upon a scaffold. She said, that she was not at her since she took that distemper, and saw her not since, but saw her on the Monday before, and her husband's daughter, and Jean Archibald in Culross; but upon the morrow the woman was troubled. James White being called, declared, that Jean Bizet was in a distemper upon Tuesday the 13th day of June, in Helen Anderson's house, betwixt 9 and 10 at night, and seemed drunk.

    3tio, That she drank not a gill in that house, but before she came to Helen's house, she was about half an hour in Mary Wilson's.

    4to, She seemed to be strangely distempered, and he heard her say, Agnes, beware lest Lilias Adie come upon you and your child.

    2d, She said to Mary Nielson, Lilias Adie thinks to use me as she used your sister.

    3tio, She complained upon Mary Wilson, but none saw the said Mary; as she went home, she cryed, now, now, Jenny, I'll be felled now, there three blew doublets, frequently, and wringing her hands. Note--She got a considerable sleep in Helen Anderson's.

    5to, As she went home, he had let her go, and she not only went freely, but did run violently, without stumbling in the least, the breadth of Torry Park, and he had difficulty to overtake her, notwithstanding there was both a dyke and furrows in the way.

    6to, He declared, that he heard that the next day she was no better.

    7no, He declared, that on the Monday before, Janet Whyte said to him, before James Alexander in Drumfin, that she would make Jean Bizet forethink what she had done to her in not paying her two barrels of ale which she sold her, on this purpose she could not get the maltman payed.

    3tio, Helen Anderson being called, declared, that Jean Bizet was in her house, out of Mary Wilson's, about 5 or 6 at night the foresaid day, and she seemed to be strangely distempered. 2dly, Her eyes raised, and could drink none. 3tio, Ater she had sleeped from 6 to near 9, and when she awaked, she cryed, by God he is going to take me! by Christ he is going to take me! O Lilly with her blew doublet! O Mary, Mary Wilson! repeating Christ keep me! Upon which Helen said to her husband, did you ever see her in this condition? He answered, never in my life, but she is too much taken up with that company, but let me to her, I shall ding the devil out of her. For this she appeals to James Tanochie and his son, She and James Whyte declares both, that they are clear to depone the same.

Agnes Henderson, wife to James Whyte, called, compeared, declared, that she was sent for to James Tanochie's wife the day foresaid, who was in a great trouble, and never saw her in the like. 2d, That she sleept a while, and when she awoke, she cryed, O God! O Christ! there is Lily coming to take me, and three blew doublets! O Mary Wilson keep me, she is coming! She adds, that Jean was in Mary Wilson's before she came to Helen Anderson's, and she said, that she desired her to go home, for Lilly will take you and the child both. She heard her say to Mary Wilson, it was not to you that she did evil, but to your sister, what aileth her at me, I never did her any ill. And as she went home, she seemed raised, but went and spak very well, and she went with her, she heard her speak often of Lilly by the way, that she was coming to take her. And she adds, that as she came first into the Newmiln, that she looked and spoke as heartsomely as ever she saw her, and seemed no way disordered; and having carried one of James Whyte's children from the Newmiln to James's house. And, on the next day, being Wednesday, she went to see how she was, and found her complaining of a sore head, and in a sweat, and she seemed not right; and she says, she is clear to depone what she has declared.

Mary Nielson being called in, said, that when Jean Bizet came to her mistress Helen Anderson her house, she was not within, but she was within when she awoke out of her sleep. 2d, She heard her say, O God! O Christ Jesus keep me! 3tio, She heard her say, O keep me! keep me! there is she coming, Lilly Adie with her blew doublet! 4to, O Mary Wilson! O Mary Wilson! 5to, She said, as she went away out of the house, she did no ill to you, but to your sister. She is clear to depone all this.

Jean Bizet being called in, declares, that on the foresaid Tuesday, she came to the Newmiln in the forenoon, carrying James Whyte's son on her back from the Craigmiln, and James Whyte was with her. 2d, She came first to Helen Anderson her house, and her husband being upon business, she went to Helen Tilloch her house. 3tio, She went to Mary Wilson's house, where Lott Nicol, with Isobel Harlay, were drinking in the room next to the door, and she went by them to the room, where Mary Wilson filled a pint of ale and desired her to drink of it. She took a drink, but did not drink beyond a gill of it; and Helen Tilloch, and Jean Tilloch, came in and drank the rest, with many others. 4to, She could scarcely have been a quarter of an hour there, and that she returned to Helen Anderson her house immediately.

Mary Wilson called, said, when Jean Bizet came to her house, she called for a choppin of ale, and stayed until that was drunk, and another was filled, and a part of that was drunk. 2d, There was none but Helen Tilloch and Jean Bizet, and herself, at the drinking of that ale. 3tio, Euphan Nicol came in, and she took a drink of it. 4to, She declares, that Jean Tilloch was not within the door then. 5to, Robert Nicol and Catharine Mitchell, and Margaret Nicol, sister to Robert Nicol, were drinking at the fire-side. 6to, She declares, that she seemeed no ways disordered with drink, nor any other way. 7no, She went up to her on Thursday afternoon, and she found her lying on her bed, and straked her head, and whether she was immediately the better of it, or not, she knew not; but she left her sitting at the fire-side with her child on her knee.

Jean Bizet says, Jean Tilloch was really there. 2d, She says it wasFriday afternoon before she settled.

Torryburn, 29th July, 1704.--After Prayer, Sederunt, Minister and Elders.

Lillias Adie being accused of witchcraft by Jean Neilson, who is dreadfully tormented, the said Lillias was incarcerate by Bailie Williamson about ten of the night upon the 28th of July.

Lillias being exhorted to declare the truth, and nothing but truth, she replied, what I am to say shall be as true as the sun is in the firmament.

Being interrogate if she was in compact with the devil, she replied, I am in compact with the devil, and have been so since before the second burning of the witches in this place. She further declared, that the first time she met with the devil was at the Gollet, between Torryburn and Newmilne, in the harvest, before the sun set, where he trysted to meet her the day after, which tryst she kept, and the devil took her to a stook side, and caused her renounce her baptism; the ceremony he used was, he put one hand on the crown of her head, and the other on the soles of her feet, with her own consent, and caused her say all was the devil's betwixt the crown of her head and the soles of her feet; and there the devil lay with her carnally; and that his skin was cold, and his colour black and pale, he had a hat on his head, and his feet was cloven like the feet of a stirk, as she observed when he went from her.

The next time she saw him was at a meeting at the Barnrods, to which she was summoned by Grissel Anderson in Newmilne, about Martinmas, their number was about twenty or thirty, whereof none are now living but herself. She adds, it was a moon-light night, and they danced some time before the devil came on a ponny, with a hat on his head, and they clapt their hands and cryed, there our Prince, there our Prince, with whom they danced about an hour.

The next time was at a meeting at the back of Patrick Sands his house, in Valleyfield, where the devil came with a cap which covered his ears and neck;--they had no moonlight. Being interrogate if they had any light, she replied, she got light from darkness, and could not tell what that light was, but she heard them say it came from darkness, and went to darkness, and said, it is not so bright as a candle, the low thereof being blue, yet it gave such a light as they could discern others faces. There they abode about an hour, and danced as formerly; she knew none at the meeting but Elspeth Williamson, whom she saw at the close of the meeting coming down by the dyke-side; and she said, she was also at another meeting in the Haugh of Torry, where they were furnished with the former light, and she saw Elspeth Williamson there also.

July 31st, 1704.--After Prayer, Sederunt, Minister and Elders.

Lillias Adie adhered to her former confession, and added, there were many meetings she was not witness to, and was at many of which she could give no particular account; and you will get more news after this. Being interrogate if she knew any more witches in the place, she replied, Agnes Currie is a witch, but she is a bold woman, and will flee upon me if I should delate her.

Being interrogate if the devil had a sword, she replied, she believed he durst not use a sword; and called him a villain that promised her many good things when she engaged with him, but never gave her any thing but misery and poverty.

The last meeting ever she was at, was 14 days after the Sacrament, in the month of August 1701, upon the minister's glebe where the tent stood, their number was 16 or 18, whereof Agnes Currie was one. She added, that she made an apology to the meeting, because she could not wait upon them all the time, being obliged to go to Borrowstouness that morning's tide. She added, that she heard Jean Neilson was possessed with a devil, and troubled with a fit of distemper, but declared she never wronged her, though the devil may do it in her likeness.

Elspeth Williamson being called, came into the prison where the session sate, and being interrogate if Lillias Adie had any envy at her, she answered, she knew no envy she had at her. Lillias being interrogate if Elspeth Williamson was guilty of witchcraft, she replied, she is as guilty as I am, and my guilt is as sure as God is in heaven.

The next time she saw the devil was about half a year ago, as she went to Culross, she saw him at the west end of the coal-fold.

Upon the affair of Janet Whyte, James Alexander being called, compeared, and declared that he never heard Janet Whyte threaten Jean Bizet in the least.

James White called, declared ut ante, but adds, that upon Friday was eight days, the 21st of July, he heard a great screeching when he was in the Craigmilne upon the bleaching green, beneath the said milne, and heard a second screech much greater, and clapping of hands and laughing, about twelve of the night, in the green on the other side of the burn; and it was observed by the bleachers to be all pastered, though there was no cloth at the burn, nor bleachers that night. Also, on the second of August 1704, Lillias declared before witnesses, that Grissel Anderson invited her to her house on that Lammas day, the morning just before the last burning of the witches. Grissel desired her to come and speak with a man there; accordingly she went in there about day-break, where there was a number of witches, some laughing, some standing, others sitting, but she came immediately away, being to go to Lammas fair; and several of them were taken shortly after, and Grissel Anderson among the rest, who was burnt, and some of them taken that very week. She adds, that Euphan Stirt warned her to the meeting at the Barnrod; and the said Euphan was burnt afterward, though she had been no longer a witch than a month before her death. She added, that she knew few of them that were at those meetings, especially the young sort, because they were masked like gentlewomen; and if Agnes Currie's heart would fall, she could tell as much as any, being in the midst of the meeting, where she saw her face by the blue low near Patrick Sands.

At Torryburn, August 19th, 1704.--After Prayer, Sederunt, &c. Minister and Elders.

Elspeth Williamson declared, that shortly after the last communion, there came a woman to her door, and bade her go east the way, whom she followed the length of the church-yard, and leaned upon the dyke, and saw a bouroch of women, some with black heads, were sitting where the tent stood. The woman that called her, went straight to the meeting, and fell down upon her knees, whereat she wondered, and hearkened if there was any reading or singing of psalms among them, and when she heard none, she thought she was in the wrong place, and did not think the woman would have taken her to the devil's meeting. She thought the woman was Mary Wilson, but is not certain; and about ten at night, some time after, a young lass came to her door, and desired her to go westward a little, whom she followed, but knew not the lass, she went so fast west the town before her, and was got the length of the Gollet or she came to the west end of the town; and when she was come west near the Gollet, she saw a meeting of women and some men, and she stood at a little distance from them, and saw them go through other for the space of near an hour, and removed insensibly eastward from her, upon which she stole away.

Lillias Adie confessed, that after she entered into compact with Satan, he appeared to her some hundred of times, and that the devil himself summoned her to that meeting which was on the glebe, he coming into her house like a shadow, and went away like a shadow; and added, that she saw Elspeth Williamson and Agnes Currie both there, only Agnes was nearer the meeting than Elspeth, who was leaning on the church-yard dike with her elbow. She added, that the devil bade her attend many meetings that she could not attend, for age and sickness; and though he appeared not to her when there was company with her, yet he appeared to her like a shadow, so that none could see him but herself. At another time, she said, that when she renounced her baptism, the devil first spoke the words, and she repeated them after him, and that as he went away she did not hear his feet on the stubble.

August 20th 1704.--After Prayer, Sederunt, Minister and Elders.

It is to be minded, that Lillias Adie appeared before the congregation on the Lord's day, and being called up by the minister and asked if she was guilty of witchcraft, she confessed freely that she was, and had entered expressly into covenant with Satan, and renounced her baptism, the devil putting one hand on the crown of her head, and the other under the soles of her feet, and she gave over all to the devil that was betwixt his two hands, and she was come hither to confess her sins, and to get her renounced baptism back again. She also desired all that had power with God to pray for her; to this the minister and elders, and whole congregation, were witnesses.

It being reported, that Agnes Currie should have delated Bessie Callander and Mary Wilson, guilty of witchcraft; Agnes being called, compeared and declared, that Robert Currie told her Elspeth Williamson told him that Bessie Callander and Mary Wilson, were witches.

George Stewart, solemnly sworn, purged of malice and partial counsel, aged 27 years, married, deponed, that Agnes Currie said to him, I'll tell you, but you must not let any of your folk know of it; he replied, I believe in Christ, I hope the devil hath no power over me. Ha, ha, said she, the devil hath done wrong to many, and he may wrong your friends or goods. Elspeth Williamson told Robert Currie, and Robert Currie told me, that Bessie Callander and Mary Wilson, are guilty of witchcraft. And this is truth, as he shall answer.--Causa scientia.

Sic subscribitur, G. S.

James Paton, solemnly sworn, purged of malice and partial counsel, aged between 22 and 23 years, depones, he was not requiring any thing of her by way of confession of persons names to which she assented in the mean time, but Agnes Currie said to him, there are two witches in Newmilne, and one of them is at the Bridgend; upon which I replied, you must tell me, for I have a sister there. Agnes replied, her name begins with a B, George Marshall replied, is that our Bessie, she answered, you are right enough, it's Bessie Callander. As to the other person, she would not tell her name at first, but said, she is be-east your house, but after owned the person to be Mary Wilson, but desired him not to divulge it to your mother or sister, least these persons do you ill. This is the truth, as he shall answer.--Causa scientia.

Sic subscribitur, JA. PATON.

George Marshall, sworn, purged, &c. ut supra, aged 39 years, married, declared, ut supra, and added, that she said, ye are husbandmen, devulge it not, least your beasts get wrang; and said to Alexander Drysdale, you go to sea, you have need to take head; and she said, the other lived be-east James Paton's house, but he going away, heard not her name. And this is the truth, as he shall answer. Causa scientia.

Sic subscribitur, G. M.

Agnes Currie assented to this in session; and that Robert Currie told her, that Elspeth Williamson told him these things; and that Mary Carmichael in Linlithgow, is a witch.

Robert Currie called, compeared, and declared that Elspeth Williamson delated to him Bessie Callander, Mary Wilson, and Mary Carmichael, as witches, which the said Elspeth referred to the probation of the witch.

The foresaid day, Lillias Adie said to the minister, that the devil was angry that she went to church, and said, that she might do as well at home. Being interrogate if he was angry like, she said, that he never looked pleasant like.--And closed with prayer.

August 29th, 1704.

Lillias Adie declared, some hours before her death, in audience of the minister, precentor, George

Pringle, and John Paterson, that what she had said of Elspeth Williamson and Agnes Currie, was as true as the Gospel; and added, it is as true as the sun shines on that floor, and dim as my eyes are, I see that.

It being reported that William Wilson knew something of Agnes Currie that was witchcraft, as also Janet Glass, they were called, and the said William declared, that about 24 years ago, Helen Johnston having overlaid her child the night after it was baptized, and the next day he was lamenting the woman's case, Agnes Currie said to him, if I had been her cummer, I could have advised her to take heed to her child; and also, that the said William was desired some time ago to bring some slyk[15] to a house that belonged to Agnes, and he answered, that his mare was in the yoke all day and could not; Agnes said she could not help it, and that same day his mare died in a stank.

Janet Glass declared, that she came once into Agnes Currie's house, having something to do with Agnes, who in the time was baking bread, and broke three several bannocks, lying in three several places, and gave it to the said Janet, and she with eating the same fell in a fever.

Torryburn, 3d of September, 1704.--After Prayer, Sederunt, Minister and Elders, except Robert Baxter, John Weir and John Wardlaw.

Agnes Currie being called, compeared, and confronted with Janet Glass; Janet declared, that about twelve years ago, she brought her cloth to her house, and Agnes was baking bread, and she broke three several bannocks that were in three several places, and gave her a piece of every bannock, and immediately she took the fever; and she adds, that she gave her a little piece of every bannock, and it was all one sort of bread. Janet declares that she is ready to swear it; also adds, Helen Lawson was so used.

Helen Lawson being called, declared, that a long time ago, Agnes Currie broke three several bannocks, and gave her a piece of every one, but she would not take the third piece; and adds, that she is ready to swear it.

Elspeth Williamson being brought in, and interrogate if she was a witch, she answered, that she would not deny that.

N. B.--Lillias Adie was buried within the seamark at Torryburn.[16]

***

William Cose being called, compeared, and owned, that on Sabbath morning, anno 1704, it being moon-light, he saw Bessie Micklejohn, or the devil in her stead, in James Chalmers's bark, then lying in Leith, and he doubts not but she saw him; and adds, that she had a green plaid about her head, as he offered to depone. The session considering that the devil appeared in her likeness, it was no proof against her, they judged it not necessary to regard that matter, and thought William Cose should not be troubled, it appearing he had not spoken it from malice, nor accused her of witchcraft formerly.

March 30th, 1709.

Margaret Humble called, declared, that Helen Key said, that when she heard Mr Logan[17] speak against the witches, she thought that he was daft, and she had up her stool to go out of the kirk: Also declared, that Helen Key threatened to strike Mary Neilson.

Jean Pearson declared, that she heard Helen Key say, that she would strike Mary Neilson. The said Helen Key confessed what all the witnesses declared.

As to the affair of Helen Key, Mary Neilson called, declared, that she heard Helen Key say, that she thought Mr Logan was not wise when he was speaking against the witches; and she had one unseemly expression that is not decent to be put on the records; and when Margaret Humble rebuked her, she answered, it was not Margaret Humble's part to speak in Mr Logan's favours, but she would not express what Mr. Logan said of Margaret Humble to her.

The session having found her convicted of prophane irreverent language against the minister and his doctrine, without any shadow of provocation, and of gross lying and prevaricating, both in private and before the session, and of threatening to strike a person because she had reported her impudent, Godless, and scandalous language,--therefore, they appoint her to sit before the congregation the next Lord's day, and to be rebuked after the afternoon's sermon.

THE END.

Footnotes:

15. Thin clay or mud.
16. Her grave is still to be seen at the west end of the town, marked with a large stone.--ED.
17. The Reverend Allan Logan, the minister, is still famous all over the country for his skill in discovering witches; and used, when administering the Sacrament, to say, "You witch wife get up from the table of the Lord," when some unhappy old woman would have risen, imagining she was pointed at, and it was well if it did not afterwards cost her her life. Daft or not, he was certainly a most wretched fanatic of the worst description.--ED.

Part V

ΔΕΤΤΕΡΟΣΚΟΠΙΑ; OR A BRIEF DISCOURSE CONCERNING THE SECOND SIGHT; COMMONLY SO CALLED.

By the Reverend Mr John Frazer, Deceased, late Minister of Teree and Coll, and Dean of the Isles;

AND Published by Mr ANDREW SYMSON, with a Short Account of the Author.
EDINBURGH: Printed by Mr ANDREW SYMSON, Anno Domini MDCCVII.

TO THE RIGHT HONOURABLE, Universally Learned, and my very Singular Good Lord GEORGE, Earl of Cromartie, Viscount of Tarbat, Lord Macleod and Castlehaven, &c. Lord Justice General of the Kingdom of Scotland, and one of her Majesty's most Honourable Privy Council,

This following Discourse, entituled ΔάτεροσκοπιαΔάτεροσκοπια, &c. written by the Reverend Mr John Frazer, late Minister of Teree and Coll, and Dean of the Isles, is, with all due respect and reverence, dedicated by the printer and publisher hereof, his

Lordship's most humble And obedient servant in all duty,
ANDREW SYMSON.

THE PUBLISHER TO THE READER.

The Reverend author of the ensuing Discourse having married my near kinswoman, and being in this city in November 1700, in order to the settling of some of his affairs. As we were discoursing of several things relating to the Highlands and Western Isles of Scotland, we came to speak of the Second Sight, reported to be so common in these parts; he told me, that as to the thing itself, it was most certain and undeniable, and that he could give many instances of it; as also, that he had written a short Discourse upon that subject. This he promised to transmit to me; accordingly, on his return home, after a tedious and troublesome voyage, both by sea and land, he sent me that Discourse, written with his own hand, desiring me to publish the same after some of his friends here had perused it: which being done, I, at my own conveniency, put it to the press, but before it was finished, I received an account that the author was dead, whereupon I forbore the publishing of it, till I should get an account of several passages concerning himself and family, designing to prefix the same to the Discourse itself, which I conceived would be acceptable to his friends, and not displeasing to the reader. And therefore I dispatched a letter to one of his nearest relations, and that was best acquainted with him, and with the passages of his life, that so I might thereby be the better informed. In answer whereunto, I received a paper containing several memoirs, from which I have collected the following account.

Mr John Frazer, the author of this Discourse, was born in the Isle of Mull, in the year of our Lord one thousand six hundred and forty-seven.

His father, Mr Ferchard Frazer, was born in the north of Scotland, near Stratharig, about the year 1606, and lineally descended of the family of my Lord Lovat, but mediately of the family of Tober, one of the Lairds of the name of Frazer.

After he had taken his degrees at the University, and applied himself to the study of Divinity, he was called by the bishop of the isles (there being then few learned men able to preach in the Irish tongue) to be minister of the Isles of Teree and Coll, (to which charge the deanry of the Isles was annext.) He was the first master of arts that preached constantly there as minister of the parish, there being then there one Ewen M'Lean, who was appointed to catechise and convene the people, there being few or none, as said is, able to serve the cure; but being there, he was very diligent in his ministerial function in teaching and instructing them, leaving them far better than he found them; for at his first coming, there were but three heritable gentlemen of the name of M'Lean that could subscribe their own names, the time Mr Ferchard Frazer served as minister of the Isles of Teree and Coll, which were conjoined in one parish, may be collected from his epitaph, written by his son, our author, which is--

Epitaphium Magistri Ferchardi Frazer Decani Insularum; qui obiit 14 die Februarii Anno Domini 1680. Aetatis 74.

> Pervigil et blandus; mitis, gravis atq. benignus;
> Doctus et Eloquii deterritate fluens:
> Pavicoves Christi pandens mysteria verbi;
> Exemplum vitæ præbuit ipse gregi.
> Luxfuerat populi lustris bis quinq. peractis,
> Sacradocens, sancto munere functus obit.
> Hic requiem tumulo corpus capit, inde regressus
> Spiritus ad Dominum, qui dedit ante, volat.
> Mr Johannes Frazerus, decanus insularum.

His mother's name was Janet M'Lean, daughter to Lauchlan M'Lean of Coll, an ancient family of that name and clan. His father, as he was careful to instruct others, so he did not neglect his son, our author, but having fitted him for the University, he sent him to the College of Glasgow, and committed him to the care of Mr William Blair, one of the regents there, who advanced him to the degree of master of arts, between the twenty-fourth and twenty-fifth year of his age. From thence he went to the Isle of Mull, and was chaplain to Sir Allan M'Lean of Duart. Thereafter, viz. March 4th 1677, he was married to Mary Symson, the only surviving daughter of Mr Matthias Symson, some time minister of Stirling, who died November 1664. Two or three years before his father's death, (being canonically ordained presbyter,) he was admitted to his father's charge, in regard his father, partly by age, and partly by sickness, was rendered very unfit to serve the cure of these two islands, Teree and Coll, as also of Icolmkiln, which was also annext to it, and at a greater distance; however, such was his care and diligence in the work of the ministry, that, by the blessing of God upon his endeavours, he converted to the true Protestant faith 24 families in the Isle of Coll, (the laird himself being then ring-leader), that were deluded by Father O'Donald and others, his father not being able to oversee his flock, by reason of his foresaid condition.

His father dying in the year 1680, he served the cure thereafter, by constant and diligent preaching, baptizing, marrying, visiting the sick, and exercising all other duties incumbent on him; but at length, because his principles would not allow all the demands of the Synod of Argyle, his charge was declared vacant, and his stipend taken from him; notwithstanding whereof, there being no minister sent to oversee these islands, he went about the exercise of his ministry as formerly, being supplied by the charity and benevolence of his parishioners, who had an entire kindness for him; but his stipend, as said is, was taken from him and bestowed some other way. And thus he continued till about a month before his death, which was on the 25th day of August 1702, in which he changed this troublesome life for a better, leaving behind him a desolate poor widow, with several children, both sons and daughters, as also a sorrowful people, who were now wholly deprived of a spiritual pastor, and of such a one as was every way qualified for that charge; for he was not only a good and learned man, but was master of their language, being born and bred up in the Isles, understood their humours, conditions, and manners of life, and being a wise and sagacious person, complaisant, and of a winning deportment; all which good qualifications he was endowed with, as all which were acquainted with him, can sufficiently testify.

As for the subject of the following Discourse, (commonly called the Second Sight) though I think it might be more fitly called the First Sight, (because it for the most part sees things before they are), I shall not undertake to defend all the notions that he has of it, and whether they will agree with true philosophy, but shall refer that to others of a higher reach and deeper understanding than I ever durst pretend to; but this I will say in his defence, that, considering the place where it was written, even among the remote Isles, vervecum in patria, where he wanted the converse of learned men, and the benefit of books, two necessary qualifications for one that writes on such an abstruse subject; I humbly conceive, that the great clerks of this age, who have the benefit of books and converse, should not superciliously undervalue him that wants them. However, although I shall not pretend to maintain all that he writes, as to the causes, &c. of this Second Sight, nor do I believe all the stories that I have heard concerning it, yet the thing itself, or that there is such a thing as is commonly called the Second Sight, I do firmly believe, being induced thereto by the relations that I have received from persons of known integrity, and such as I suppose are wiser than to be imposed upon, and honester than to impose fables instead of truths, upon others. Among the relations that I have been told concerning this subject, I shall only single out one or two, and then I shall conclude.

A noble peer of this nation being one morning in his bed-chamber, and attended by several persons, when his servant had put a new coat upon his Lord, a gentleman standing by, presently cry'd out, for God's sake, my Lord, put off that coat; and being asked the reason, he replied, that he saw a whinger or poinard, stick in the breast of it. The noble peer esteeming this as a mere fancy, replied, 'this coat is honestly come by, and I see no reason why I may not wear it.' The gentleman still entreated, and earnestly craved, that it might be put off: upon which debate, the noble peer's lady being not far off, came in, and being informed of the whole affair, intreated her Lord to comply with the gentleman's desire, which he did; mean time one of the servants standing by, desired the lady to give it him, and he would wear it. She granted his request, who put it on, and ere night he was stabbed by a poniard, in that very place which the gentleman had pointed to in the morning. This relation I had from a very ingenuous and understanding gentleman, who was grand-child to the said noble peer.

    I shall add another strange story, which I had from a reverend minister of the gospel, and my intimate acquaintance. 'Tis thus--In the year 1665, Alexander Wood, eldest son to the Laird of Nether Benholm, in Angus, having ended his prentiship with a merchant in Edinburgh, told Mr James Walker, that (in the year 1662 or 1663), he had been employed by his master to go to the Lewis to make up herring; and being there, and having a good tack of herring, their salt and casks were all made use of, and then they being idle, he began to fret that his master had delayed so long to supply them; and being one day drinking in a country house, and complaining, he went to the door of the house, and there followed him a country man, who said to him, If you will give me a small hire, I'll tell you what is become of the ship you are looking for; and without more ado, he set his foot upon the gentleman's foot, in which time he saw the ship in a great storm, ready to perish, and the seamen casting out their lading to lighten the ship; but when the country man's foot was off his he saw nothing. The ship at that time was about 100 miles from them, and about 48 hours thereafter, she came into the same harbour, and had been in the same condition he saw her in at that time the country man's foot was on his foot. It would be tedious to add any more stories that I have had from persons of undoubted veracity; and therefore, Reader, I shall only subscribe myself

Your humble servant in all duty,
ANDREW SYMSON.

A SHORT ADVERTISEMENT TO THE READER.

COURTEOUS READER,

You may be surprised to meet with such an abstruse theme (handled in specie by few or none), from the pen of a person in my circumstances, lying at a great distance from the Universities and centre of the kingdom, and consequently may be justly supposed to want that ordinary help of books and conference with the learned, that others may enjoy.

In the first place, believe that I am so far from affecting vain singularity, (a hateful vice in the schools as well as the pulpit), that nothing of that kind moved me to treat of the subject of the following Discourses. But for my own satisfaction I drew up the following heads, and did not resolve at the first to expose them to public view, (justly fearing the censure of presumption); but I was, by the persuasion of some serious friends, prevailed with to commit myself to the favourable judgment of the learned, (who might sooner commend my endeavours than censure my failings), rather than suppress such a fine subject, which probably might be more fully and largely treated of by others after the perusal of this Discourse. Take this pamphlet then in the rude dress that I could give; at least it may excite thy thoughts, if not to approve of what is here deduced, yet to propone of thine own a more satisfying method of explaining this remarkable phenomenon, which is the genuine design and wish of,

SIR, Your humble servant,
The AUTHOR.

ΔΕΤΤΕΡΟΣΚΟΠΙΑ; OR, A BRIEF DISCOURSE CONCERNING THE SECOND SIGHT, Commonly so Called.

EDINBURGH, Printed by Thomas Webster.

Many have undertaken to treat of the nature and operation of Spirits; as also of the various manners of divination among the Gentiles, (and but too much used among Christians,) likewise of the perturbation and deception of the fancy, caused by melancholy; and very many speak in ordinary discourses of this called the Second Sight, and the consequences of it, but none that I know handle it in titulo.

That such representations are made to the eyes of men and women, is to me out of all doubt, and that effects follow answerable thereto, as little questionable. But I have found so many doubt the matter of fact; which I take to be the reason that so little has been written of it, that I think it necessary to say something briefly, that may put the existency of it beyond all scruple. If I should insert all the clear instances that I have had of this matter, it would be tedious and unnecessary, therefore I will content myself, and I hope will satisfy the reader, with four or five instances, as follows.

The first instance is by a servant of my own, who had the trust of my barn, and nightly lay in the same. One day he told me he would not any longer lie there, because nightly he had seen a dead corps in his winding sheets straighted beside him, particularly at the south side of the barn. About an half year thereafter, a young man that had formerly been my servant, fell dangerously sick, and expecting death, would needs be carried near my house; and shortly thereafter he died, and was laid up a night before he was buried in the same individual barn and place that was foretold; and immediately the servant that foretold this came to me and minded me of the prediction, which was clearly out of my mind till he spoke of it.

The second instance is after this manner. I was resolved to pay a visit to an English gentleman, Sir William Sacheverill, who had a commission from the English Court of Admiralty, to give his best trial to find out gold or money, or any other thing of note, in one of the ships of the Spanish armada, that was blown up in the bay of Topper-Mory, in the Sound of Mull. And having condescended upon the number of men that were to go with me, one of the number was a handsome boy that waited upon my own person; and, about an hour before I made sail, a woman, that was also one of my own servants, spoke to one of the seamen, and bade him dissuade me to take that boy along with me, or if I did, I should not bring him back alive; the seaman answered, he had not confidence to tell me such unwarrantable trifles. I took my voyage, and sailed the length of Topper-Mory; and having stayed two or three nights with that liberal and ingenuous gentleman, who himself had collected many observations of the Second Sight in the Isle of Man, and compared his notes and mine together, I then took leave of him. In the mean time, my boy grew sick of a vehement bloody flux,--the winds turn'd cross, that I could neither sail nor row,--the boy died with me the eleventh night from his decumbiture,--the next morning the wind made fair, and the seaman to whom the matter was foretold, related the whole story when he saw it verified. I carried the boy's corps aboard with me, and after my arrival, and his burial, I called suddenly for the woman, and asked at her what warrant she had to foretell the boy's death; she said, that she had no other warrant but that she saw, two days before I took my voyage, the boy walking with me in the fields, sewed up in his winding sheets from top to toe, and that she had never seen this in others, but she found that they shortly thereafter died; and therefore concluded that he would die too, and that shortly.

The third instance was thus. Duncan Campbell, brother-german to Archibald Campbell of Invera, a gentleman of singular piety and considerable knowledge, especially in Divinity, told me a strange thing of himself. That he was at a time in Kintyre, having then some employment there, and one morning walking in the fields, he saw a dozen of men carrying a bier, and knew them all but one, and when he looked again, all was vanished. The very next day, the same company came the same way, carrying a bier, and he going to meet them, found that they were but eleven in number, and that himself was the twelfth, though he did not notice it before; and it is to be observed, that this gentleman never saw any thing of this kind before or after, till his dying day. Moreover, that he was of such solid judgment and devote conversation, that his report deserves an unquestionable credit.

The fourth instance I had, to my great grief, from one John M'Donald, a servant of Lauchlan M'Lean of Coll, who was then newly returned from Holland, having the charge of a captain. This gentleman came one afternoon abroad to his past-time in the fields, and this John M'Donald meets him, and saw his clothes shining like the skins of fishes, and his periwig all wet, though indeed the day was very fair; whereupon he told privately, even then, to one of Coll's gentlemen, that he feared he should be drowned. This gentleman was Charles M'Lean, who gave me account of it. The event followed about a year thereafter, for the Laird of Coll was drowned in the water of Lochy in Lochaber. I examined both Charles M'Lean and John M'Donald, and found, that the prediction was as he told me; and the said M'Donald could produce no other warrant, than that he found such signs frequently before to forgo the like events. This man indeed was known to have many visions of this kind, but he was none of the strictest life.

The fifth instance is strange, and yet of certain truth, and known to the whole inhabitants of the Island of Eigg, lying in the latitude of 56 degrees 20 minutes; and longitude 14 degrees. There was a tenant in this island, a native, that was a follower of the Captain of Clanrannold, that lived in a town called Kildonan, the year of God eighty-five, who told publicly to the whole inhabitants, upon the Lord's day, after divine service, performed by Father O'Rain, then priest of that place, that they should all flit out of that Isle, and plant themselves some where else; because that people of strange and different habits, and arms, were to come to the Isle, and to use all acts of hostility, as killing, burning, tirling, and deforcing of women; finally, to discharge all that the hands of an enemy could do; but what they were, or whence they came, he could not tell. At the first there was no regard had to his words; but frequently thereafter, he begged of them to notice what he said, otherwise they should repent it, when they could not help it; which took such an impression upon some of his near acquaintance, as that severals of them transported themselves and their families, even then; some to the Isle of Cannay, some to the Isle of Rum. Fourteen days before the enemy came thither, under the command of one Major Ferguson and Captain Pottinger, whilst there was no word of their coming, or any fear of them conceived. In the month of June 1689, this man fell sick, and Father O'Rain came to see him, in order to give him the benefit of absolution and extreme unction, attended with several inhabitants of the Isle, who, in the first place, narrowly questioned him before his friends, and begged of him to recant his former folly and his vain prediction; to whom he answered, that they should find very shortly the truth of what he had spoken, and so he died. And within 14 or 15 days thereafter, I was eye witness (being then prisoner with Captain Pottinger), to the truth of what he did foretel; and being before-hand well instructed of all that he said, I did admire to see it particularly verified, especially that of the different habits and arms, some being clad with red coats, some with white coats and grenadier caps, some armed with sword and pike, and some with sword and musket. Though I could give many more proofs, as unquestionable as these, yet I think what is said, is sufficient to prove the being of such a thing as the same in hand; and I cannot but wonder, that men of knowledge and experience should be so shy to believe that there may be visions of this kind administered by good or bad angels; there being nothing more certain, than that good angels suggested visions to the prophets of the Lord, before the coming of Christ in the flesh, and particularly to the apostle St John, after the ascension of our Lord; likewise that evil angels presented visions, as well as audible voices, to the 450 false prophets of Ahab; the 400 prophets of the Groves, is as little to be doubted; it being as easy, if not easier, to work upon the sight, as well as upon the hearing. We know but too well, that necromancers and magicians themselves, have not only seen the shapes and forms of things, but likewise have allowed others to see the same, who had no skill of their art. A precedent for which, is the Witch of Endor.

    I remember, about 23 years ago, there was an old woman in my parish, in the Isle of Teree, whom I heard was accustomed to give responses, and likewise averred, that she had died and been in heaven, but allowed to come back again. And because she could not come to church, I was at the pains to give her a visit, attended with two or three of the most intelligent of my parish. I questioned her first whether she said she was in heaven; and she freely confessed she was, and that she had seen Jesus Christ, but not God the Father, or the Holy Ghost; that she was kindly entertained with meat and drink, and that she had seen her daughter there, who died about a year before;--that her daughter told her, though she was allowed to go there, that she behooved to come back and serve out her prentiship on earth, but would shortly be called for, and remain there for ever. She could very hardly be put out of this opinion, till I enquired more narrowly of her children, if she fell at any time in a syncope; which they told me she did, and continued for a whole night, so that they thought that she was truly dead; and this is the time she alleged she was in heaven. The devil took an advantage in the ecstasy to present to her fancy a map of heaven, as if it had been a rich earthly kingdom, abounding with meat, drink, gold, and silver. By the blessing of God, I prevailed with her to be persuaded that this was but a vision presented to her fancy by the devil, the father of lies; and that she might deprehend the falsehood of it from this one head, that she imagined her body was there, as well as her soul, and that she did eat and drink, and was warmed, while, as her own children, and the neighbours that watched her, did see, and did handle her body several times that night, so that it could not be with her in heaven. I did further examine her what warrant she had for the responses she gave, which were found very often true, even in future contingent events. She freely confessed, that her father upon his death-bed, taught her a charm, compiled of barbarous words, and some unintelligible terms, which had the virtue, when repeated, to present, some few hours after the proposition of a question, the answer of the same in live images before her eyes, or upon the wall; but the images were not tractable, which she found by putting too her hand, but could find nothing. I do not think fit to insert the charm, knowing that severals might be inclined to make an unwarrantable trial of it. This poor woman was got reclaimed, and was taught fully the danger and vanity of her practice, and died peaceably about a year after, in extreme old age.

I know assuredly, that Janet Douglas, that was first a dumbie, yet spoke thereafter, who had given many responses by signs and words, and foretold many future events, being examined by Mr Gray, one of the ministers of the city of Glasgow, denied any explicitor implicit paction, and declared freely, that the answers of the questions proponed to her were represented by a vision in lively images, representing the persons concerned, and acting the thing, before her eyes. This Mr Gray exchanged several discourses in write with Sir James Turner, concerning her.

By this time, you may see that this theme deserves the consideration of the learned: First, to enquire how much of this may come from a natural constitution and temperament, when confounded with a flatuous or melancholic distemper; and what influence an external agent, namely, an angel, good or bad, may have upon the organ of the eye and the fancy, and how far the medium between the organ of the eye and an object visible, may be disposed for their purpose, namely, the air and light; and what connexion may be found betwixt the representations made to the eye or fancy, and the future contingent events that experience teaches do follow thereupon: as for example, a man is seen bleeding, or sewed up in his winding sheets, who is shortly to be wounded, or assuredly to die.

As for the first, all the learned physicians of the world know too well by experience what great labour they have to cure the deceptions of the fancy, especially in hypochondriac diseases; nay, patients cannot be persuaded but they see men, women, fowls, and four-footed beasts, walking abroad or in their chambers. Seldom it is, that a man passes any great and turbulent fever, without the trouble of some such representations. It is memorable, that a gentleman, that had been a great proficient in physic himself, imagined at length that there was a quick frog in his belly; and after he had travelled over a good part of Italy, and consulted with the doctors of Padua, yet could not be cured, or dissuaded. He came at length to the learned physician Platerus, in Bazil, who told him, that a frog by certain experience is known not to live above three years, so that his distemper continuing longer than three years, could not be caused by the frog, that could not live so long. Moreover, that his stomach would strangle the frog, and that the frog could not live any considerable time out of its own element, the water; so that the properest and most specific medicines being made use of, it were a shame for him to be so obstinate. At last he was persuaded, and his fancy satisfied. This story is no less renowned of what befell Andreas Osiander, a man learned in most languages. When he was a young man, and being troubled with a quartan ague, a little before the fit he could not be persuaded that he was in the house at all, but that he was in a wood, and much molested with wild beasts and serpents of all kinds; neither could he be prevailed with that this was false, till Facius Cardanus was called for to him, who cured him for the time, so that he knew his friends that were sitting beside him, and the chamber to be his own chamber; but after Facius had left him, he was troubled with the same opinion and distemper, even till the ague had quiet him. I have myself seen a neighbour of my own, and my parishioner too, John M'Phale, that lived to the age of fourscore years, a man that was truly very sagacious by nature; and though his sight was much decayed, the seat of his judgment was nothing touched; and as he grew weaker, merely by old age, without any remarkable distemper, I made frequent visits to him. One day as I was coming away from him, he told me he had something of consequence to ask at me, and desired all to remove except his wife and another gentleman, that was a friend of his. This done, Sir, says he, I desire to know by what warrant or commission so many of my friends, that are dead long ago, are allowed to come and discourse with me, and drink before me, and yet are not so civil as give me a tasting of it? I told him, that it was only the trouble of his fancy, and his frequent thinking of the world to come and his friends that were gone before him; and he replied to me very smartly, Sir, says he, I perceive it is the work of the fancy, for since I cannot see yourself, (for only by your voice I know you) how could I see them? It was strange that he saw them the very mean time that others were in the house with him, and asked several questions at them, but got no answer. And, for all this, the seat of his wit was as entire as ever: moreover, this trouble left him a little before he died.

Many such illusions are reported of eremites, caused merely by the confusion of the brains, bred by their fasting and unwholesome food, which I shall not trouble the reader with.

If you will ask how cometh this to pass, take notice of the following method, which I humbly offer to your consideration. Advert, in the first place, that visible ideas, or species, are emitted from every visible object to the organ of the eye; representing the figure and colour of the object, and bearing along with it the proportion of the distance, for sure the objects enter not the eye, nor the interjacent distant tract of ground; and a third thing different from the eye and the object, and the distant ground, must inform the eye. These species are conveyed to the brain by the optic nerve, and are laid up in the magazine of the memory, otherwise we should not remember the object any longer than it is in our presence; and a remembering of these objects is nothing else but the fancies reviewing, or more properly the soul of man, by the fancy reviewing of these intentional species formerly received from the visible object unto the organ of the eye, and reconducted unto the seat of the memory. Now, when the brain is in a serene temper, these species are in their integrity, and keep their rank and file as they were received; but when the brain is filled with gross and flatuous vapours, and the spirits and humour enraged, these ideas are sometimes multiplied as an army, by mist; sometimes magnified, sometimes misplaced, sometimes confounded by other species of different objects, perhaps by half and half, so that the fancy has two for one, one bigger than two of itself, and sometimes the half of one and the half of another, represented in one; and this deception is not only incident to the fancy, but even to the external senses, particularly the seeing and hearing; for the visus, or seeing, is nothing else but the transition of the intentional species through the crystalline humour to the retiform coat of the eye, and judged by the common sense, and conveyed by the optic nerve to the fancy.

Of this we have a clear demonstration from the representation of external objects through a crystal in glass, upon any lucid, smooth, and solid reflectant, placed before the glass in a dark chamber, which is one of the noblest experiments in the whole optics.

Now, if these species formerly received and laid up in the brain, will be reversed back from the same to the retiform coat and crystalline humour as formerly, these is in effect a lively seeing and perception of the object represented by these species, as if, de novo, the object had been placed before the eye; for the organ of the eye had no more of it before, than now it has; just so with the hearing, it is nothing else but the receiving of the audible species to that part of the ear that is accommodated for hearing, so that when the species are retracted from the brain to their proper organs, for example, the ear and the eye, hearing and seeing are perfected, as if the objects had been present to influence the organs de novo. And it is not to be thought that this is a singular opinion, for Cardanus, an eminent author of great and universal learning and experience, maintains this reversion of the species, and attributes his own vision of trees, wild beasts, men, cities, and instructed battles, musical and martial instruments, from the fourth to the seventh year of his age, to the species of the objects he had seen formerly, now retracted to the organ of the eye, and cites Averroes, an author of greater renown for the same opinion. See Cardanus de subtilitate rerum pagina trecentesima prima.

And it seems truly to be founded upon relevant grounds. I have observed a sick person, that complained of great pain and molestation in his head, and particularly of piping and sweating in his ears, which seems to have been caused by the species of piping and singing which he had formerly heard, but were now, through the plethory of his head, forced out of the brain to the organ of the ear, through the same nerves by which they were received formerly; and why may not the same befall the visible species as well as the audible? which seems to be confirmed by the optic experiment. Take a sheet of painted paper and fix it in your window, looking steadfastly to it for a considerable time, for example, some few minutes, then close your eyes very strait, and place a sheet of clean paper before your eyes, and open your eyes suddenly, you will see the painting almost as lively as they were in the painted sheet with the lively colours. This compression of the eyes by consent, causes a compression of the whole brain, which forces back the visible species of the painted sheet to the organ of the eye, through the optic nerve, which will presently vanish, if the reflectant did not help to preserve them. You may see then how much of these representations may be within ourselves, abstracting from any external agent or object without the eye, to influence the same.

The second thing that comes under consideration is, the influence and operation of external agents, namely, an angel, good or bad. It is not to be denied, but good angels may help and dispose all our faculties, excite, elevate, and set them upon edge and action; likewise, that evil angels may perturb, confound, and hurt, our external and internal senses, (when permitted) particularly by stirring the spirits, humours, and vapours, which of themselves, when so stirred, help to make many shapes and representations, either regular or irregular, (as has been formerly observed) and withal, they can colorate external objects far beyond any painter, insensibly to the beholder, repente applicando activa passivis; and that they can alter the medium interposed between our senses and the objects, by making it grosser or thinner, opaque or lucid, is a thing not to be questioned. For a clear proof of this I hope any rational man will allow me.

That even the evil angels, who were created in a degree above us, must have a more penetrating wit than ours is, and having experienced from their creation, to this very day, and can be present to every experiment found out, or that is committed to writing by the art of man; and withal, being not subject to oblivion as man is, (for they have no material faculty to be obliterated), I say any rational man will allow me, that they can do as much, and beyond what the art of man is able to do; but so it is, that painters can make one object more pleasant than another, distorted and worse favoured than another,--that any smoke may engross the air,--that a cloud removed on or off the face of the sun, give way to the beams of it to illuminate the air, or to eclipse its light,--that vapours and exhalations, from sea and land, multiply and magnify objects, misshapes and distorts them, and makes them of diverse figures, all in an instant, which is observable in hot summer days, especially in the end of the canicular days, for you may readily see about three or four in the afternoon, the same hills (providing they are situated at a considerable distance from you) to be of diverse shapes, forms, and figures, changing very suddenly from one shape to another, for example, from a globe to a pyramid, from a pyramid to a quadrangular figure, &c. All which our ordinary multiplying, magnifying, and distorting glasses, produce. Moreover, that physicians can administer such medicines as may provoke a man to madness and rage, yea, to fantastic or hypochondriac fits; so also medicines that move pleasant and unpleasant dreams, by exciting the melancholic or sanguine humours, raging or peaceable dreams, by moving the choleric or phlegmatic humour.

How much more can the prince of the air do, and his retinue, who is better seen in the nature of the elements and their compounds; who is better seen in the nature of trees, plants, minerals, stones, the secret qualities of springs and fountains, rivers and lochs, and the influence of celestial bodies, &c. and who is better seen in the constitution of every man, his customs and inclinations, and his present state and bygone circumstances; I say, in all these, he is better seen than any man, and can accommodate them to his purpose beyond the greatest virtuosos.

Let us therefore consider, that an evil angel being permitted thereunto, can muster in our brain the latent intentional species of external absent objects, and can present the same to the fancy in the methods best fitting his purpose, and not only so in time of our sleep, (for then indeed the fancy sticks with more tenacity to what it apprehends), but also when we are not sleeping, he can deduce these species by forcing them out of the rooms or cells of the brain, to the organ of the eye and ear, and so of necessity a man either sitting or going in the high-way, will hear and see such things as these species do represent; and seeing that naturally it may be done, as would appear from what is above spoken from the strength and force of medicines to operate upon the spirits and humours of man to work strange things, why may not a good or bad angel excite nature to it? or by an immediate impulse force these material qualities to the organs of the external senses, as well as they can move their vehicles, which are the spirits and humours.

The third thing proposed was, the connexion of these representations with the future contingent events that are observed to follow them, as for example, a second sighted man sees a winding sheet upon his neighbour, or blood running down his face, shoulders, or arms, he concludes that he must die, or be wounded in the face, shoulders, or arms. If you will ask what warrant he has for this, he will tell, he has found by experience, that whenever he saw the like of this, that he found death or wounds to follow. Quaeritur, then, what connexion can this representation have with an effect or contingent event not yet existant? For answer to this, God, who knoweth all things, no doubt imparteth much of the foreknowledge of things, not only to good angels, but also evil angels, for reasons well known to himself, particularly that they might give some true signs, and so have way to deceive in many things besides; and though the signs foretold should surely come to pass, it does not infer that the doctrine of evil angels, and their lies that they would suggest to mankind, should be credited. This is clear from the 13th of Deuteronomy, 1, 2, and 3, verses, If there arise among you a prophet, or a dreamer of dreams, and giveth thee a sign or a wonder, and the sign or the wonder come to pass whereof he spake unto thee, saying, let us go after other gods, (which thou has not known), and let us serve them; thou shalt not hearken to the words of that prophet, or that dreamer of dreams, for the Lord your God proveth you, to know whether you love the Lord your God, with all your heart, and with all your soul. And this is very just with God when men give themselves over to a reprobate and wicked mind, and evil and unwarrantable practices, expressly against the Lord's commands; I say it is just with God to let evil angels or spirits delude them, and give way to these spirits in order to confirm their lies; to appoint signs before hand, which signs, by God's appointment, may come to pass, answerable to the prediction. It may rationally, and very probably be concluded, that Ahab's false prophets, in number 400, have often foretold truth; and this purposely by God's appointment, that they might be the better believed, and more easily persuade to lay siege to Ramoth Gilead; and it is hard to conceive that Ahab should give them so much credit, or they themselves so extraordinary confident, if they had not had many truths suggested to them, and made proof of the same to Ahab. It is not for nought that we are commanded to try the spirits, and that rather by their doctrines, than their signs and wonders, or fair and smooth pretences. Therefore, suppose these evil angels to know a contingent future event, either by a revelation, or natural or moral causes, they may, in the method foresaid make the representation of them to the eyes or ears; as for example, an angel, good or bad, finds that either the lungs, heart, stomach, liver, or brain, are under such a consumption, as may against such a time kill a man; or that he knows the secret contrivance of a potent party that is resolved to wound or kill him, or that it is revealed to him it should be so (which may very well be, as has been above noted), he can easily represent these before hand, though the event should follow but a considerable time thereafter; he has no more to do than to reverse the species of these things from a man's brain to the organ of the eye.

Here ariseth a question from what has just been said, whether it be more probable that good angels make this representation (because men having this second sight are found to tell truth, and to be innocent in their lives, and free of any paction, either implicit or explicit, likewise free of any fraudulent design, and sound enough in the necessary articles of their salvation), or that it be done by evil angels for the trial of men and women, juggling with their fancy and external organs, and so have a patent way to tell lies among some truths. For answer to this question, I shall not be ready positively to determine these things, but I humbly conceive, that as the representations are oft done by evil angels, so likewise it is probable that it may be done by good angels. I cannot be so uncharitable to several men that I have known to be of considerable sense, and pious and good conversation, as to conclude them to be given over to be deluded continually by an evil angel: Moreover, I conceive that there are many good Christians, if they would advert well, that have some secret tokens and signs of notable alterations to come, suggested to them before hand; and that these signs, some of them are common to them with others, as dreaming, which are often observed to be completely fulfilled, and that some of the signs and warnings are peculiar to some persons, which fail not to answer to the things signified; as for example, I have certainly known a man, that when he found an unvoluntary motion in such a member of his body, particularly his right hand or right eye, that was sure that some matter of joy would shortly come to his hearing; and that if he found the same motion in the left eye or hand, it signified infallibly grief: And that which is more wonderful, the thing to come signified by these signs and warnings keeped an exact proportion with the continuance or vehemency of the motion; if the motion continued long, so did the joy or the grief; if the motion was snell or vehement, so was the matter of grief or joy; and finding that this man was both a good man, and of a right penetrating wit, and had art enough, it moved me to use freedom with several other good men that had knowledge and sense enough to examine circumstances to a hair. I found very many to acknowledge the very same thing, yet signified by different signs, (which shows they are not signa naturalia, but ex instituto), which puts me in mind of Dr Brown's observation to the same purpose, in his inquiry into vulgar errors, where he concludes several presentations to be acted in us by our tutelary angels that have the charge of us at the time. Mark this, though the signs be different in themselves, yet to each particular person, his own sign is still significative of the same thing; and why might not this of the second sight be counted amongst one of these? I likewise humbly conceive, that God might compense the want of many other gifts to poor men, by giving them this minor sort of knowledge. But I would advise all of them that have the second sight, to examine themselves, and to pray earnestly to God that no evil angel should have power to abuse their senses, because the devil still strives to imitate what God, or his good angels, communicates to his own children. I know that the common opinion of some philosophers and divines will be objected, and that is, that angels, good or bad, may condense the air, figurate and colorate the same, and make it of what figure or shape they please, so that this representation is made by external objects in effect emitting visible species to the eye; and consequently, that it is not the reversion of the species formerly received; though, as I have observed before, that good and bad angels can alter the medium in a strange way, and can work great alteration on the elements and their compounds, I think it very improbable that any created power can bring the air to that solidity, and actually condense it, colorate, and figurate it, as to represent a man by a beast, or Peter by Paul, especially at such a distance as from one side of a chamber to the other. The miracles done by the magicians of Egypt is their Achillean argument; but in short, I say, that what was done by the magicians of Egypt, has neither been a delusion of the senses, (as some would have it) much less that the devil could produce the creatures de novo of condensed air, and that for the following reasons: First, thence it would follow that Moses and Aaron were deluded as well as the Egyptians; but the last is false, therefore the first: Secondly, it would follow, that the fashioning and framing of Adam's body of clay, was but a mean act of creation in comparison of these creatures, if they should be fashioned and framed of condense air, which is naturally a fluid element, not so easily stigmatized as the earth. I do not deny but the devil can snatch dead and quick bodies from one place to another, and that insensibly to the beholders, by pressing their optic nerves, as Franciscus Valesius has observed in his Sacra Philosophia, and I conclude with Abraham Couley, (no contemptible author) that the magicians of Egypt were after this manner served by the devil, to imitate God's power in the hands of Moses and Aaron. Mark, finally, if it were within the sphere of angelical power to take bodies of condense air, what needed them assume such material and earthly bodies as these angels that came to Abraham and Lot assumed? whose bodies could be touched and handled, and whose bodies were not found to yield to the touch, as the most condensed air must do; and it is very consisting with reason, that the angels, good or bad, should rather assume bodies of the element of the earth, which is a great deal more easily brought to the figure and fashion of a body, than the air. Some curious spirits, perhaps, may desire to know whether this second sight be hereditary or propagable from father to son; and I think no wonder that some would think so, because the sanative gift of the king's evil is lineally traduced to the natural heirs of the crown of England; and there is a whole family in Spain, that has a sanative gift of some particular diseases, which gift is propagated from the father to the son; neither is it diminished or augmented by the morality or immorality of the persons, as has been observed by that famous philosopher and physician, Franciscus Valesius, who lived in that kingdom, and had time and opportunity to examine the truth of this affair. In short, I answer, that it is not propagable from father to son, neither peculiar to any particular family; and as I have observed many honest men, free of all scandal that ever I could learn, to have it; so I have observed many vicious persons to have it who foretold truth oft enough.

Perhaps it may be doubted what should make this second sight more frequent here than in the heart of the kingdom; I answer, that it is the lack of observation and inquiry that it should not be found there as well as here. Secundo, that it passes under a great odium and disgrace with the most of men, which causes those that see it, conceal it. Thirdly, I confess that credulity and ignorance give occasion to evil spirits to juggle more frequently, than otherwise they would have done. But sure it is, that men of little learning and education may be recompensed by notable presentations, not so obvious to others of greater parts. I remember of a nobleman in Spain, that was deaf and dumb from his infancy, and yet was taught by a monk to speak, and understand what was spoken to him, only by observing the motion of his lips that spoke to him. Sir Kenelm Digby saw him, as he tells in his Treatise of Bodies, and the monk that taught him, was a cousin of Franciscus Valesius. This was more than ordinary sagacity and docility, and it is found, that many dumb persons foretel many things before hand, and it is a hard measure to conclude all to be from evil spirits. In fine, as I noted before, as questionless Satan may, and often does, deceive after this manner, so it is as sure, it may be allowed, that good angels may forewarn this way, as well as by other signs and tokens, as Dr Brown observes.

It is observed, that those who have the second sight, have this representation at any time of the day, but indeed more ordinarily in the morning and evening, and with candle light.

The design of these weak conceptions on this sublime theme, is not to impose upon any man, freely leaving every man to follow his own judgment in things that offend not church or state, but that others of greater capacity may be stimulated to prosecute the same in a better method, humbly submitting myself to the judgment of my betters, to whose hands perhaps this pamphlet may come.

FINIS.

www.ingramcontent.com/pod-product-compliance
Lightning Source LLC
Chambersburg PA
CBHW032050090426
42744CB00004B/161